Praise For
Being There Without Going There

"Virtual teaming is becoming a mainstream practice because of the needs of global enterprises to coordinate work activities across boundaries of time, space, and cultures. But many enterprises fail to meet management and employee expectations in virtual collaboration by neglecting critical leadership and management processes. *Being There Without Going There* provides a comprehensive set of insights into virtual leadership, management, and the enabling technologies required to support this growing workstyle. The authors depart from the usual 'how to' approach and embed best practices and principles in the context of an actual fictional account of companies that launch a successful virtual teaming initiative. This technique bridges the gap between theory and practice and makes both the benefits and risks of virtual teaming a reality for the most skeptical business reader."

Michael Bell, VP and Research Director, Gartner Inc.

"Technology investments must demonstrate their business value quickly, and in hard dollar terms. This book shows how to use emerging Internet Collaboration Tools to substantially reduce time to market and cost."

Ray Lane, General Partner, Kleiner, Perkins, Caufield and Byers

"This book presents an interesting and thoughtful depiction of the virtual company. Any manager with even a marginal appreciation of organizing through the internet should read it."

Gordon Walker, Professor of Strategy at Southern Methodist University

"The global banking industry is under pressure to work more efficiently. This book is a guide on how to get you global IT staff to work as one team and to leverage offshore resources more effectively."

Merritt Lutz, Advisory Director, Morgan Stanley, Chairman MSIT Holdings, Inc.

BEING THERE WITHOUT GOING THERE

BY GEORGE AND KEITH VAN NESS

ASPATORE
C-Level Business Intelligence™

Published by Aspatore, Inc.
For corrections, company/title updates, comments or any other inquiries please email info@aspatore.com.

First Printing, 2003
10 9 8 7 6 5 4 3 2

Copyright © 2003 by Aspatore Books, Inc. All rights reserved. Printed in the United States of America. No part of this publication may be reproduced or distributed in any form or by any means, or stored in a database or retrieval system, except as permitted under Sections 107 or 108 of the United States Copyright Act, without prior written permission of the publisher.

ISBN 1-58762-319-6

Managing Editors, Robyn Gearey & Alicia Abell

Material in this book is for educational purposes only. This book is sold with the understanding that neither any of the authors or the publisher is engaged in rendering medical, legal, accounting, investment, or any other professional service. For legal advice, please consult your personal lawyer.

This book is printed on acid free paper.

A special thanks to all the individuals that made this book possible.

The views expressed by the individuals in this book (or the individuals on the cover) do not necessarily reflect the views shared by the companies they are employed by (or the companies mentioned in this book). The companies referenced may not be the same company that the individual works for since the publishing of this book.

BEING THERE WITHOUT GOING THERE
TABLE OF CONTENTS

Preface	7
Chapter 1: The Challenge	13
Chapter 2: The Existing Operation	25
Chapter 3: An Alternative Model	41
Chapter 4: How Indonesian Medical Technologies Works	49
Chapter 5: Communication and Relationships	63
Chapter 6: Guiding Principles	75
Chapter 7: Business Travel	83
Chapter 8: Getting Started	89
Chapter 9: The Home Court First	105
Chapter 10: The New Business Processes	115
Chapter 11: Picking Projects	133
Chapter 12: Early Implementation: Lessons About People and Processes	139
Chapter 13: Managing Across Department and Corporate Boundaries	161
Chapter 14: Managing the Extended Enterprise	177

Chapter 15: Mergers and Acquisitions and Offshore Development   199

Chapter 16: In Summary: How Virtual Should You Be?   225

PREFACE

How would you like to:

- Visit clients in three different cities
- Work directly with suppliers and partners on two continents
- Reduce time to market by 25 percent
- Reduce costs by 10 percent
- And still make it home in time for dinner?

Making these possibilities a reality for you is what this book is about.

The world is global. It is no longer possible for companies to build a single campus and manage the entire enterprise from that location. Winning companies will leverage better relationships with their customers and suppliers, as well as better use of a global labor force. They will create real access to their field organizations from their headquarters. As the labor force continues to be made up of dual-income families and aging baby boomers, winning companies will learn to think differently about their labor force. This book is for the executives, managers and employees of those companies.

- Executives will see that distributed organizations make money. If you are already running a distributed team, use this book as an instruction manual on how to use processes and technologies to make that distributed organization come together as one team.
- Software executives who have struggled to realize the economic benefits of offshore development will learn the steps to make that work.
- Line managers tasked with running distributed teams will learn about Internet-based distributed technologies and management processes and how to explain to management why these types of changes require top-level attention.
- Employees will learn to show management how to let them participate on projects regardless of where they live and work, allowing them to balance lifestyle with employment.
- Highly skilled baby boomers will find a way to seek the alternative lifestyles of semi-retirement while continuing to contribute valuable skills to their companies, stay stimulated and earn a good living.

- Technologists who already understand the mechanics of distributed teams will be able to use this as a reference source to show management a new state of the possible that can enhance their careers and career options.

So what's different today?

During the 1990s, thought leaders behind the Internet revolution promised a digital world, where everything would be automated and you could do and get everything from home. The reality is that we still get caught in traffic commuting to and from work. Every year, businesses spend even more money on travel expenses. Top people in key labor markets still command top dollar while critical positions go unstaffed. All this while companies could solve their cost and time-to-market problems if they could only work more closely with their partners and do more in low-cost labor markets such as India.

The original developers missed one critical piece: the person on the other end. Websites permit interaction with content, but not with real people. If the next step in the evolution of communications can occur, great leaps in productivity will follow.

The first step in global communications was the printing press. As soon as that was invented, literacy, once the privilege of the wealthy, became available to everyone. The next steps were radio communications, the telegraph and the telephone. Now people could effectively communicate across distances. Our current economy and, in great part, our society, are the result of these evolutions in communications.

Today, thanks to the Internet, information can be sent from one side of the planet to the other across corporate boundaries in under seven seconds. Data stored on a server can be accessed from anywhere. E-commerce permits buyers and sellers everywhere to find one another quickly and easily.

So what is the missing piece?
The ability to interact with the person on the other end

We tried it once. It was called "video conferencing." It was supposed to enable us to work together as if we were in the same room together. Only it didn't work very well.

The reason for the limited success of video conferencing becomes obvious… once you think back to the first step in the communications revolution: the printing press. The most important communications are always written down. We send memos. We write business plans. We write software. Then we sit down at a table and look at the written document together. Businesses do not need a way to see each other's faces across thousands of miles. But they do need a way to work on the same document together across thousands of miles.

PREFACE

While the Internet revolution was taking place, the most important developments were slipping quietly to the side: data conferencing tools, Internet-based meeting centers, hosted document databases, instant messaging and touch-screen solutions. With these tools, you can scatter a team to the wind, and still get people to work as if they really are in the same room together.

Don't believe it? Here's just one of countless examples:

A software company needed a venture capital proposal Monday morning, but only had the weekend to build it. Conventional wisdom says to fly the team to a central city and work nonstop over the weekend. This company did it a little differently.

All relevant documents were placed in a central database. Regular meetings took place across the Internet, so that everybody could work together on the documents being produced. Between meetings, individuals worked on their pieces of the proposal, and then uploaded the results on the database for the next meeting. During meetings, team members merged the pieces and edited them with the full input of all members of the team *as if they were in the same room together.*

At one point, the team determined a need for an extra person to support some of the subsidiary work being produced. On short notice, an additional member was called in. He was told what was expected, where the information was stored and the time of the next meeting. *The new member of the team was a full participant less than 15 minutes after the call.*

The team beat the deadline, and they did it from six different cities: San Francisco, Calif.; Ontario, Calif.; Dallas, Texas; Fort Worth, Texas; New York, N.Y. and Virginia Beach, Va.

Want to be this effective?
Read this book!

Chapter 1:
The Challenge

Ray is the head of product development for a major division of Alpha Corporation, whose revenue is slightly over $800 million. He's been with the division for over 17 years and has been head of product development for just over three years. Right now, the company is in the midst of the second year of an economic downturn, which the division has navigated reasonably well. While most competitors have experienced substantial losses and decreases in revenue, Ray's division has actually grown revenue slightly while allowing margins to dip only minimally. In fact, the division is the second best in a large corporation. Overall, Ray and his colleagues look forward to the return of the good years, when product development funds flowed freely and the greatest challenge was hiring good product managers and engineers at any price.

At the moment, Ray is sitting with Sandra, his number-two, talking about the new division president, Marvin. Marvin came from the only division of the company that has outperformed theirs in the downturn. As might be expected, people have greeted Marvin's arrival with mixed emotions. They look forward to the success he will bring to the division, but they fear his reputation as an impatient, no-nonsense manager. They worry he will demand substantial changes that might affect the culture that they have developed—one that has produced solid success, year after year.

Ray tells Sandra that he has his first one-on-one meeting with Marvin today. "So far, we've only met in division staff meetings," says Ray. "Marvin talks glowingly about our product development teams, but I'm not sure where he is going to want us to go from here. From what I hear, he's been pretty tough on sales, manufacturing and logistics. Some people are expecting him to put his own lieutenants in charge of those operations."

Sandra reminds Ray that their division has a track record of getting the best products to market faster than the competition—and with designs that yield exceptional quality. "Marvin has already acknowledged that," she points out.

Ray nods his head, but somewhat reluctantly. "I guess you're right, Sandra," he says. "I'm just nervous because I know he's demanding, and I don't know what to expect. Well, I'm off to see him and find out what he has in mind. See you in an hour or so."

Shortly afterward, in Marvin's office, Ray waits for Marvin to return from a meeting. Marvin enters with a burst of energy. "Ray, sorry for

The Challenge

making you wait," he says. "It's great to finally get some time with you. I wanted to have this meeting sooner, but I really needed to spend time with sales and marketing to get renewed energy into that team. This recession has been hard on them. We also need to take a hard look at manufacturing and the supply chain. They are both operating all right, but they need to be a lot better if we are going to stay competitive and really start to drive growth."

Marvin then launches into an animated monologue, talking about how in an economic downturn, the best companies gain market share. He notes that while Alpha Corp. has gained share during the current downturn, the gain hasn't been nearly as large as it should have been. Marvin believes the company can and should put out new products faster than ever before, replacing its competitors in key accounts and acquiring struggling middle market companies that can make components for existing products or expand Alpha Corp.'s most profitable product lines. "Then we can use our strength in the market to become the clear and present market leader forever," he says.

"More important, as the market recovers, we need to hold these disciplines so that we stay the tightest-run operation in the market and convert that operation to growth and profit. The chairman wants a very profitable, $3 billion division in four years, and I've committed to make that happen," Marvin concludes.

"That's a great vision and well within our reach," responds Ray diplomatically. "The management team is looking forward to working with you to get that done."

"Well, Ray, everything I've seen so far indicates that product development is the crown jewel in this division."

Ray relaxes visibly. "Thanks, Marvin. We have a really dedicated team that has built some great products and some great processes that we can use for new products. You can depend on us to continue to produce for you."

Then Marvin takes Ray by surprise. "I appreciate that Ray," he says, "but if we're going to dominate this market, I need more than that." He says that he wants to talk to Ray about some substantial changes he wants made in both product development and sales and manufacturing.

Ray notes that the management talent in his division is strong, so any acquisitions should be easy to handle. "What other kinds of changes were you thinking about, Marvin?" he asks.

Marvin tosses out a presentation. "Well Ray, I've already talked to the chairman about a half a dozen changes that I think would really position us for the future. I want to get to work with you on what I have in mind for product development right away."

Marvin explains that his first concern is the product launch cycle, which looks a little ragged to him. The last two products the company put to market could have gotten there a lot faster, he thinks. "We had the product ready to manufacture almost two months before we had the marketing material!" he exclaims. But from the day the product was ready to manufacture, it took more than a month to get the supply chain up to speed—and then almost 90 days to get the field sales force ready to sell the product. Marvin shakes his head. "With a product development cycle that lasts, on average, 12 months, we waste at least 90 days of revenue. We can produce at least a 20 percent improvement in time to market. That would generate real revenue impact," he says. By his calculations, 90 additional days of full production revenue on the last product launch would have increased total revenue by almost $20 million this year alone.

Barely stopping to take a breath, Marvin moves on to his second point. According to a recent customer survey, customers wish the company would interact a lot more closely with them so that they could give feedback on products and revisions. "We sell a high-end product, and our biggest customers expect to be able to talk to our engineers and product managers," Marvin says. "We need to get out of the labs a bit more and get in front of the customer." If the division can do that, he says, the sales department has agreed to be accountable for an increase of at least 5 percent in revenue per account, with only a small increase in commission cost.

Ray leans back. "I completely agree, Marvin. Our team has ideas on how to do both of those things. The only problem is that we've suggested some of those changes before, and we haven't always been able to get the funding."

"Dynamite!" Marvin continues. "Glad you mentioned funding. I've looked at our cost structure relative to the best-in-class engineering teams in similar industries. We are 10 to 12 percent more expensive than the top three teams. We need to take the next 12 months to look for ways to stay the highest quality team while making our engineering team the low-cost producer." According to Marvin, if product development can reduce its engineering costs by 12 to 15 percent, it will have the investment capacity to integrate acquisitions and to fund growth, as well as to improve product release cycles or even invest in another product line. "I know that will take time," he says, "but we need to get our product development per revenue dollar to the position of clear market leader in the next 12 months."

Marvin then mentions how, in previous acquisitions, the company has moved the new engineering teams to one of its main campuses. But the organizations the company is currently examining will be hard to acquire under those circumstances, so it's likely that Ray will need to run a much more distributed engineering team. According to Marvin, the company needs to learn how to integrate new acquisitions without relocating engineering teams, all the while reducing the cost of each acquisition.

THE CHALLENGE

"Ray, if we can do these things this year, then no one else in the industry will be able to touch us," Marvin asserts. "As the market recovers, we will have an insurmountable lead."

Ray leans forward with his elbows on his knees and says, "Let me see if I have this straight: Keep quality and innovation high, while taking 20 percent out of the product launch cycle time and 12 to 15 percent out of costs in an organization that is already stretched thin. Then integrate four acquisitions over a year without moving them to one of our engineering campuses. Sounds like a tough challenge."

"It is a tough challenge, Ray, but that's what it takes to be the clear leader," Marvin responds. He tells Ray that he didn't just make these goals up; he's actually studied competitors and organizations from other benchmark industries and found examples of companies that have achieved similar goals. Marvin also mentions that he knows a consultant, Chris, who will have some suggestions to help Ray's team meet the goals he's outlined.

"But this is going to mean abandoning some of our usual practices," cautions Marvin. "You can only tune your existing model so far. Chris is an expert at running distributed teams. He helped me do things like break down the barriers between product development and the other individuals in the launch process when I worked in my last division. He also helped us make a lot better use of our distributed teams and leverage real cost and time savings by having the team distributed around the world. He's got a couple of model companies he works with that are getting better results than we're even aiming for."

Marvin hands Ray Chris' card, cautioning that Chris won't be the total solution to what product development will need to do, but that he'll be a good resource to start with. Marvin then suggests that he and Ray talk every few weeks about what Ray is learning and what kind of support he needs to reach his goals. "Then we'll start talking about the range of things your team does and ways to make more money by doing less," Marvin says. "If we kill a few of our low-potential product investments, we can rededicate the best engineers to the highest-revenue projects. Chris can't help you with that, but I can."

Ray rubs his head. "Well, it's a tough order, Marvin," he says, "but your data says it can be done. Our team is already worked to the bone, and it's going to be a hard sell to convince people we can do even better, but we'll keep an open mind as we look at what Chris suggests." Ray ends the meeting by saying he'll call Chris today. He also tells Marvin he'll put together a team, led by Sandra, to examine opportunities for improvement in product development, especially in integration of new acquisitions.

Back in Ray's office, Sandra asks how the meeting went.

"Well, 'interesting' is probably the best description," Ray responds. "Marvin says that product development is the crown jewel of the company, but he wants a few changes."

He then stuns Sandra with the news that Marvin wants the division to keep quality and innovation high while taking 20 percent out of the product launch cycle time, reducing product development costs by 12 to 15 percent and integrating four acquisitions without moving them to one of the company's campuses—all over the next year. "I told him I would make you the task force leader to come up with recommendations," he informs Sandra.

"You're kidding, right?" Sandra asks. "Ray, our people have been doing more with less for the past two years. There isn't much more water to squeeze out of this rock."

Assuring her that he's not kidding, Ray tells Sandra about the data comparing their company to the best in class, and how there is clear room for improvement. He also tells her that Marvin has suggested they contact Chris, a consultant Marvin used while leading his last division, who should be able to help them in their quest to run distributed teams and integrate acquisitions.

"Here's his contact information," says Ray. "Why don't you give him a call and see if we can set up some time with him? Meanwhile, clear your calendar. I'm going to make you the leader of this project, and it's going to take a lot of your time. Marvin is fair, but if you and I don't produce the best team in the industry, then our replacements will."

Chapter 1 Takeaways

- The market is tough, but the winners will grow anyway.
- There is a new way that companies can squeeze an additional 20 percent out of time to market and 12 to 15 percent out of costs. This book will show you how.

Chapter 2:
The Existing Operation

A few days later, Sandra and Ray meet with Chris. Ray thanks Chris for being available to see them so quickly and asks if he has had a chance to see the product development center. Chris responds that Sandra has already taken him on a tour, as well as briefed him on the product development team and its processes.

"It's an impressive team," Chris tells Ray. "I can see why Marvin wants to make it the nucleus of his new business plans."

Ray thanks him for the compliment but expresses concern about meeting Marvin's ambitious goals, which Sandra has outlined to Chris. "Well, Marvin never did set easy goals," Chris responds. "That's why he has been as successful as he is. But he also knows that if you set the bar too high, people will think they can never get over it—and Marvin doesn't achieve his success by burning up his teams, moving on and leaving a mess for the next guy to fix. So, I imagine that he's looked at the facts and believes his goals are attainable. In fact, I've already noted a few potential areas for improvement in my early discussions with Sandra."

Ray bristles a bit at this, saying he thinks his team is pretty well-oiled as it is but that he's willing to listen to what Chris has to say. His only request is that Chris provides some practical advice, not just expound on theory.

"Great," says Chris. "I think I can do that for you." First, however, he'll need some additional information about the product development operation, he says. Chris' first set of questions addresses cost: He knows the team spends about $140 million a year on product development, but he wants to know exactly where that money goes. "Does it mostly go to salaries, or are there a lot of other costs?" he asks.

"Well, the money pays for people, but about 30 percent of it pays for contractors, outsourced services and consulting companies, not salaried employees," says Ray. He explains that his team's head count and projects are split across three campuses, with about half the work done in Detroit, where Ray and Sandra are located, another 30 percent done in London and the balance done in California.

"OK, when you staff individual projects, do they get done in a single location, or are they done by teams that are distributed across all three of your locations?" asks Chris.

Ray says that for the most part, teams in a single location staff his projects. Splitting a project across two locations creates too many travel costs and too many communication problems.

Chris then asks if Ray always has the right people for every project at a single location. And if not, how does he solve that problem?

"Well, I suspect by the way you asked that question, you know that we don't," Ray responds. He explains that when the right people aren't available at a single site, the company either pays for them to travel or, if the project is a long one, relocates them for the duration of the project. If neither of those options works, Ray hires someone new or uses a contractor.

Chris probes a bit more. "Do you suppose that you have everyone at every site working on the most important projects, or do you have some people working on 'B' priorities while an 'A' project is going unstaffed in a different center? Or is the 'A' project being staffed by a person who isn't right for a key role?"

Ray acknowledges that employees aren't always used in optimal roles, but explains that the company simply can't move people around the country every time it starts a new project. "So where is this whole line of questioning going?" he finally asks.

"Bear with me for just a few more questions; then let me summarize some thoughts," says Chris. "OK?"

Ray nods his head. "Sure, although I'm still not sure where all this is going," he says.

Next, Chris asks about turnover. Is Ray losing people he can't afford to lose because of lifestyle decisions or other personal reasons, such as a spouse getting transferred?

Actually, product development lost one of its best product designers just last month because his wife took a great new job in San Diego, Ray says. It's going to cost almost $100,000 to recruit and train a replacement, and the team will lose a month or two of work on an important product, he adds. "But if you hire great people from two-income families, this kind of loss is just the way things are," Ray says.

Chris finishes up his questions about cost with some queries about software, which the company embeds in a lot of its projects. Where does software development take place, he asks? Does any of it occur in offshore locations, such as India, where employees cost only 20 to 30 percent as much as they do in places like Detroit and London?

The Existing Operation

"No," says Ray. "We tried that, but people in India work at an entirely different time of day, and we had major communications problems as a result. By the time we developed and explained the specifications, we could have been nearly done with the software."

After scribbling for a few more seconds on his notepad, Chris looks up at Sandra and Ray and smiles. "OK, so let's consider some areas where you could be spending excess money," he says. He then highlights the following:

- Employees are working on low-priority projects because there isn't a top-priority project located in the center where they're working.
- Contractors are hired in one center to do work that could be done by under-utilized, full-time employees in another center.
- The company pays travel and relocation expenses for people who are assigned to projects at a site away from their home base.
- Work time is wasted due to time spent getting to and from various sites.
- Contractors cost $120,000 a year to work at one of the company's established centers when the same work would cost $40,000 a year in India or the Philippines.
- Turnover costs nearly $100,000 per employee because of the need to hire and train replacements for people who leave the company due to a spouse changing jobs, a newborn baby, a sick family member or another lifestyle issue.

"If we could find ways to get your people assigned to all of the right projects, and then let them work from wherever they are, no matter where the project is, how much do you think you could you save on staff, travel, turnover and contractors?" Chris asks.

"Millions," responds Ray, "but how are we supposed to do that?"

Chris again asks Ray to suspend his disbelief for a few minutes while they make a list of areas worth examining. Ray shakes his head, saying he'll play along for a while longer, but that he still doesn't see the value of the exercise.

"Ray," Sandra jumps in, "Chris and I have talked about some of his ideas, and they really do seem possible, maybe even practical. Let's hear him out for a while."

"OK," grumbles Ray, "but I'm an engineer. I need proof."

"That's a fair challenge," Chris acknowledges. If he can provide examples of other companies that are succeeding at making the changes he's talking about, will Ray agree to consider trying some of them?

"Sure. Marvin shouldn't leave me in my job if I refuse an offer like that," Ray says.

The idea, explains Chris, is to make a significant dent in the 12 percent cost savings target by allowing Ray to find the best and least expensive talent that can do the necessary work, and then making that talent productive without moving people around all the time. "It's having them 'be there without going there,'" Chris says.

Making Acquisitions

Chris then asks a few questions about a different subject: time to market and time to integration for newly acquired companies. He tackles the acquisitions first. "Do you know the companies that Marvin is currently targeting for acquisition, their products and their locations?" he asks.

Because Marvin and the mergers and acquisitions team are still shopping around for companies, Ray and Sandra aren't sure yet. "They keep that sort of thing pretty close to their vests until we get into due diligence," explains Ray. Nonetheless, he is able to confirm that most of the target companies won't be in the same cities as Alpha Corp.'s three product development centers.

"What's the reason for the acquisitions?" Chris asks. "Are they for the technology and the markets, or for the people?"

In his experience, says Ray, Alpha Corp.'s acquisitions are usually for both purposes. Many young companies have great products and great talent, he explains, and if Alpha Corp. gets the products but loses the talent, a lot of that valuable synergy is lost in the acquisition.

"So you want to save the talent, but that means not relocating people to one of your development centers, right?" asks Chris.

"Exactly," responds Ray.

Chris' final line of questioning about acquired companies concerns the actual products they will bring to the table. Are the products completely stand-alone, or will they be integrated into Alpha Corp.'s core product lines? For example, will the acquired companies be making sub-assemblies or even final assemblies that are used in other products?

Because Ray doesn't know who the companies are yet, it's hard for him to say. But given some of the conversations he's been part of at management meetings, he assumes that the new companies would be fairly integrated. "I know that's what the M&A team is looking for," he explains.

"So," asks Chris, "if you are going to acquire companies, integrate their products and retain their people without moving them, is it safe to say that your travel time and costs will be high—unless you can find some way to get the teams together to work every day 'virtually,' without making them get on airplanes every Monday and Friday?"

Ray nods.

"Ray, I would call that a compelling event," says Chris. He then goes on to explain that Ray and Sandra are going to have to increase the work between centers no matter what they believe about reducing costs in their core product development areas. "We need to solve that problem, and then see if we can leverage it back to help us with the first set of questions about cost," he says.

"I guess when you put it that way, you're right," says Ray.

Chris then moves on to what he promises will be his last topic: time to market and the product development and launch cycle. Who are the stakeholders in the product development and launch cycle? he asks. And why did they not come together as seamlessly as Ray would have liked during the last few product launch cycles?

Ray answers the question about stakeholders first. The major stakeholders are executive management, product management, marketing, engineering, quality assurance, manufacturing and, to some degree, sales, he says.

Chris asks about people who work in purchasing and logistics, who need to make sure that raw materials are in the pipeline. Ray adds them to the list.

What about people from outside the company? Chris mentions suppliers, transportation companies and sub-contractors. Are any of them stakeholders as well?

"Sure, we have all of those," says Ray. In fact, the last product was partially developed by a company that Alpha Corp. was buying, he explains. Until the acquisition was complete and the government had approved the deal, the acquired company needed to be treated like a sub-contractor. "Then all of a sudden they were part of the team and we had to deal with them differently," Ray says. "That probably cost us a month right there."

"OK, so why didn't it all come together?" Chris asks.

A lot of it had to do with coordinating project plans, Ray says. Every team would have a project plan, and although individual teams got together frequently to compare their plans, the day after they had a meeting, something would change. "Keeping the plans up-to-date became a nightmare," he says.

Chris asks if all of the teams working on the last product launch were in the same location.

The company's manufacturing centers are frequently in low-cost locations that aren't close to development headquarters, Ray explains.

The Existing Operation

Marketing teams are in a variety of different countries, and sales people are spread all over the world.

Could a few months of the product launch slip—and some of the extra costs—have been avoided if all of the teams had somehow been brought together in a single, easy-to-maintain plan, with a single program manager in charge? Chris asks. Would regular team meetings to compare designs and schedules and to discuss issues have helped?

"Yes," says Ray, "but the teams were all over the place, so we couldn't meet all that often." Travel time and expense meant that the teams could only get together in one room every so often. As for holding regular meetings? "You might as well grab the sun and stop the wind," says Ray.

"That's where you're mistaken," responds Chris. "Marvin knows that there are ways to think and act as a distributed team, and by doing so, a smart, talented division like yours can really get to the next level. In short, it's all about communications."

He then shows Ray and Sandra a diagram on his laptop.

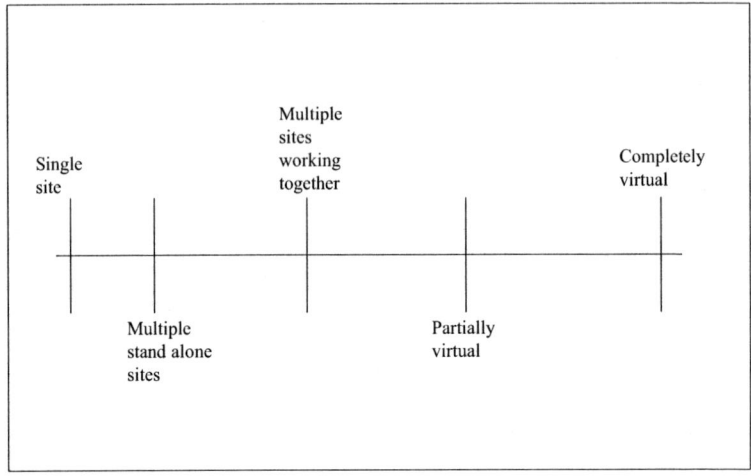

Chris explains that every company lives somewhere on this spectrum: from the far left, a single-site headquarters, to the far right, a company without walls or boundaries. "The reality of our global economy is that very few companies can stay on the far left for very long," Chris says. In fact, he believes that Alpha Corp. is actually at the second line—multiple stand-alone sites—and moving rapidly toward the third because of its acquisition strategy.

At the same time, Chris explains, it doesn't always make sense to try to move all the way to the right and act as an entirely distributed company. "It takes a long time to get used to that model, and companies that have people who have worked in the single-site paradigm for many years take longer to make the transition to virtual."

The Existing Operation

The real goal, Chris says, is to look at the existing business in detail and determine how much the company can really benefit by becoming distributed and over what time frame. "I'll suggest a few new technologies, but it's really about changing the way people think and operate," he says.

Then Chris responds to Ray's earlier challenge to show him a company that is making this kind of distributed model work. He says he'd like to introduce Ray to the young CEO of an international company, Indonesian Medical Technologies (IMT). "She happens to be coming to Chicago next week for an annual gathering of friends. I'm pretty sure that I can get her to spend some time with you and talk about her company's virtual model," Chris says. Then, after looking at her company and the state of the possible, Chris and Ray can go back and look at Ray's business.

Then, Sandra, Ray and Chris can decide what they need to do to get multiple sites working together so that Ray can execute his acquisitions integration, Chris says. Next, they'll consider how to drive those techniques home to get a big chunk of the 12 percent cost savings and to fix the time to market around product launch. "Then you can take Marvin up on his promise to help you get the rest of the cost savings by looking at making more money by doing fewer projects," Chris says. "At that point, you will have moved from being a great product team to a world-leading product team that other people will study."

"Well, I'm far from convinced," says Ray.

"Fair enough. Are you convinced enough to go to Chicago for a day?"

"Sure."

CHAPTER 2 TAKEAWAYS

Companies often spend excess money on the following:

- Employees who work on low-priority projects because there isn't a top priority project located in the center where they're working
- Contractors who are hired in one center to do work that could be done by under-utilized, full-time employees at another center
- Contractors who cost three times as much to work at one of the company's established centers as they would if the were in India or the Philippines
- Travel and relocation expenses for people who are assigned to projects at sites away from their home base
- Turnover costs due to the need to hire and train replacements for people who leave the company due to a spouse changing jobs, a newborn baby, a sick family member or another lifestyle issue

In addition, work time is wasted by time spent getting to and from various sites.

However, there are ways to think and act successfully as a distributed team. The key to moving toward a successful virtual model is improving communication among teams in various locations. Changing the way people think and operate, along with some new technologies, are key.

Chapter 3: An Alternative Model

Chris and Ray are sitting on the patio of a resort outside of Chicago. Sandra has remained at the office to do some planning and research. As Chris and Ray sip coffee, a young woman walks around the corner. "Chris, it's good to see you," she says. She turns to Ray. "Is this the guest you were telling me about?"

"Yes, it is. Li, meet Ray."

"Ray, it's a pleasure to meet you," she says. "How's business?"

Ray shrugs. "Pretty good, all things considered."

"Chris told me some of your story. What kind of challenge has your boss handed you to get you on a plane to Chicago on such short notice?"

Once again, Ray outlines the task ahead of him. "Well, I'm supposed to squeeze 12 to 15 percent out of product development costs, reduce time to market by 20 percent and prepare to integrate four new acquisitions—all the while maintaining our existing quality standards."

"Wow! That's quite a challenge. Imagine what you'll be worth when you get there!" exclaims Li.

At first Ray has a blank look on his face; then he breaks into a chuckle. "You're right, but how am I supposed to do it?" he asks. "I mean the whole thing is a huge communications problem."

Li smiles. She says that in her opinion, the only way for Ray to achieve these goals is to get all of his employees to act like they're in the same room together—like they're part of the same team.

"Exactly!" responds Ray. "Chris tells me that your company does that every day. I can't even get teams in separate departments and on separate floors to work together. How in the world does your company do it?"

Li draws up a chair and tells Ray the story of Indonesian Medical Technologies. The company has over 200 employees, offices in 14 countries and manufacturing operations in three countries. According to Li, the company's costs are well below industry average; annual revenue is $30 million, with a nearly 60 percent growth rate. "At our current

An Alternative Model

course and speed, we expect to go public in the next 12 to 18 months," she says.

The company has two basic lines of business. Its initial focus was doing outsourced design and manufacturing for companies that had good ideas and strong sales and marketing channels but were looking for low-cost, high-quality engineering and manufacturing to supplement their core teams. While IMT did have one product that it took to market itself, outsourcing was really the model that got it to about $12 million in annual revenue, Li says.

More recently, the company has begun to develop more of its own patents, she says, and is beginning to develop its own direct sales and marketing channels. It's a higher-risk business model, but Li thinks IMT is ready for it. Besides, it offers much faster growth and higher profit margins than the outsourcing business.

"So where does your success come from?" asks Ray.

Li thinks IMT's success boils down to two things: its people and its somewhat unique business model. "We are able to attract some of the best talent in the world by hiring people wherever they are, and then letting them live pretty much any lifestyle they want," she says. IMT hires people in every labor market in the world, not just expensive engineering centers such as London, San Francisco and Frankfurt. This allows the company to keep its pool of talent high and its costs low—almost 30 percent lower than peers in its sector, in fact.

Having employees scattered all over the world gives IMT some other advantages as well, says Li. Working virtually allows the company to locate manufacturing and prototyping operations in low-cost markets where it gets government incentives to build facilities. And perhaps most important, her teams work 24 hours a day by passing work from engineer to engineer using what she calls a "follow the sun" engineering method.

IMT's broad geographic spread not only allows it to leverage the global economy for engineers and manufacturing, but also enables it to maintain close access to customers and the latest research. "For a small company, we have a very good network of contacts that we keep constantly in place," says Li. And because many of IMT's design engineers live close to customers and to some of the world's most innovative universities and medical customers, the company can constantly maintain and extend that network.

"That's interesting," says Ray. "Chris showed me some of your sample projects and their financial results before we got here, so it's hard to argue with your outcomes. But they seem to be sort of one-of-a-kind. Conventional wisdom holds that a company this distributed simply can't work." Ray then goes on to cite numerous academic studies that show that a team's productivity is directly linked to the distance between people's desks.

Entire business architectures have been built around the concept of moving people into proximity to the team they're working with, he says. "Now, would you have me believe that all of those studies are invalid, and that your company is living proof? What do you do differently, and can it be replicated? Do you have specialized tools and techniques that no one else knows about? Do you have a secret army of process experts and behavioralists locked in a closet somewhere?"

According to Li, IMT doesn't have any secret weapons; it just leverages a few standard communications tools better than most. She reminds Ray that the majority of the studies he's talking about looked at traditional companies with traditional processes—and poor use of new tools. She also cites a major university study from the early '80s that showed that students wrote better papers if they wrote them by hand and entered them into a computer later. "Can you imagine a businessperson or a student working that way today?" Li asks. "For new processes to work, you have to adopt and learn new technologies, become effective with those technologies and then use them to create business practices that continue to leverage the state of the possible. We think we've done that, and our results prove us right," she says.

"All right," says Ray. "I'll suspend disbelief for a while, but you don't mind if I remain skeptical, do you? Tell me about some of these Web technologies you're talking about and how they encourage new ways of thinking."

Li then outlines some of the tools that her teams use on a regular basis:

- Interactive meeting management software such as WebEx or Net Meeting
- Project collaboration environments such as Lotus Notes, Microsoft SharePoint or the Business Engine Network
- Electronic whiteboards such as Smart Technologies
- White-boarding on PCs using touch-screen PC surfaces
- Occasionally a Web cam
- Instant messaging software such as Microsoft Instant Messenger

"Wow, that's quite a list," says Ray. "Isn't it expensive and difficult to train your people to use all those tools?" he asks.

"Not really," says Li. She reminds him that IMT is a small company that has been using these tools since it started. Also, because all of the tools run on the Internet, connecting them is easy and inexpensive. IMT spends about $7,000 when it hires a new employee and about $3,000 a year so that person can work remotely. Those costs are even less if the person chooses to work in one of IMT's offices, says Li. "That's not much to pay if it allows you to assemble and motivate the best engineers in the world and make them more productive than any company in your space," she adds.

Li then cites some evidence of how much money her company is saving:

An Alternative Model

- IMT's staff and office costs are 30 percent below industry average.
- Employee retention is almost 100 percent because people not only love their work, but it also fits nicely into their lifestyles.
- Relocations costs are avoided, and the company doesn't lose employees if they move to another city for personal reasons.
- Business travel costs are low because there is usually an IMT employee somewhere reasonably close by, anywhere in the world.
- Recruiting costs are exceptionally low because people tell others about IMT. Search companies are rarely necessary, even for the most mission-critical roles.

"OK," says Ray. "So tell me how this all plays out. Where do your people actually live and work? How do you run your projects? How do the tools you mentioned help?"

"That's a lot of questions," says Li. "Let's see if I can answer them one at a time."

CHAPTER 3 TAKEAWAYS

Here are some keys to success for IMT, a fully distributed company:

- The company does an exceptional job of leveraging communication tools such as instant messenger, project collaboration databases and Internet meeting managers.
- It understands and expects that success will be measured by results, not time spent in the office.
- It accepts and embraces the promise of the virtual workplace, which means that everyone shares the same vision and expectations. No one says, "It can't be done."

CHAPTER 4:

How Indonesian Medical Technologies Work

Li begins by giving Ray an overview of the company structure. IMT has small offices in eight cities, although only about half of IMT employees work in an office. The rest of the team works from home. Li explains that the company learned early on that there are two kinds of people. The first type needs a structured workplace where it is quiet and there is daily physical contact with colleagues. The second type can slip on a headset, log onto the meeting center, call a peer and work from anywhere at any time. Some live near universities where they get a lot of stimulation. Others live in the mountains or at the beach, and some are parents who work from home while the kids are at school and then again in the evening after the kids go to bed. A few are people who would have retired but for the alternative work style that lets them stay in the labor force—and add tremendous value to the company.

"OK," Ray says, "so you believe people can work from anywhere. How do they do that? Don't they need to get in a conference room and brainstorm like other engineers? You must spend a fortune flying people in to start projects, solve problems and hold status meetings!"

No," Li responds, "in fact, we have a very low travel budget. The tools we discussed allow us to meet remotely as effectively as if we were in the same room together." She then walks Ray through a typical project.

IMT uses a project collaboration environment where everyone working on a project can store essential information: the project plan, status reports, issues that need to be resolved, brainstorming notes, work product from the team, stuff from other projects and even discussion notes. Every project begins with a plan in the collaboration environment—sometimes just a few lines, other times more complex. From then on, everything about the project is stored in one place so everybody can find it. That way, every member of the team can see the plan, what they are supposed to do and the work of the other project members. The value really becomes apparent as you manage across time zones. One project member can be 12 hours away from another, but still see everything that was accomplished that day and what needs to happen next.

IMT also uses Internet meeting software. This tool facilitates electronic meetings during which participants can share and see exactly what is on each other's computers. One person can be showing a presentation on a projector in a conference room, with another colleague attending the meeting from her desk 1,000 miles away. She can still see and hear everything that anyone in the meeting room can see and hear. Coworkers can even create or walk through a design drawing just as if they were leaning over the same conference table.

Since each person is sharing the same view of a document or other application on his computer screen, everyone can see the cursor. Each person can use the mouse to point at things or to ask a question. Anyone in the meeting can take control to make a point, just like using a laser pointer in a presentation, Li explains. The same tools also allow any meeting participant to make changes to the document or drawing that is being discussed. If everyone agrees, the changes are stored as a new version in the collaboration database so that everyone can see the new version.

"We do a lot of team meetings," Li says. "Sometimes it's the whole team; sometimes it's just two or three engineers working together to solve a specific problem." When there's a problem, she continues, they put together a conference call, launch an instant meeting and go to work, just like a traditional team would walk into a conference room. That allows IMT to assemble teams from anywhere in the world and get people to work together as if they were within 50 feet of each other.

"Except it's a virtual 50 feet, not a physical 50 feet." Li says. Then, the teams can do shift work by taking advantage of time zones as well. That's the "follow-the-sun" methodology, Li explains. Based on this infrastructure, IMT has built structured work processes, just like in an office. When people are given tasks, they get an assignment walk-through to make sure they understand the task and the work they need to produce. And problem-solving sessions can happen any time, Li points out.

"Interesting. Why use a collaboration database rather than just emailing the work to one another?" Ray asks.

"That would be horrible!" Li exclaims. "Imagine if you pulled up the wrong copy of something and spent the day working on the wrong version. A project collaboration database is really organized, so we let it keep track of things. When I finish, I store my work as a new version. Then you can call it up and work on it and store your version as well. The database keeps both versions so we know what we changed. We can even go back and restore an earlier version if we don't like the changes one person made. You can't stay that organized on email."

"What about meetings?" Ray asks. "How do you use a computer with a phone in your hand? Alternatively, if everyone is on speaker phones, it must make the office noisy."

"That's what a headset is for," says Li. "You just slip on a phone headset and your hands are free." For example, one of her engineers has his phone and his computer connected to wireless controllers in his home. He goes out and sits in the sun by the pool while he attends design meetings. "Now tell me, how will anyone ever recruit him away from me and get him to commute to an office again?" she says, smiling. "In fact, instead of driving two hours each day, he works an extra hour on his projects and feels like he is ahead of the game, and still gives us an hour more than before. It's really productive."

Ray looks perplexed. "OK, but how do you brainstorm? Every engineering team that I know has a room where the walls are covered with flip charts that only they can understand. How does someone in another city look at the charts?"

Li explains how electronic whiteboards work. An electronic whiteboard is essentially a large touch-screen display and software that allows the user to take an electronic pen and write on it just like a real whiteboard or flip chart. When that person is also using an Internet meeting manager, others can see what's being written from his or her PC. Because the tool is digital, users can change pages and make a roomful of flip charts, just as they could if they were in the same room. The whiteboards can then be stored in the collaboration database, so that all members of the project team can get to them anytime they want.

"No scanning, no transcribing, no losing pages," Li says. A team can even store several versions in order to keep track of what has changed during the project, when it changed and who changed it.

Li continues. "Since all the plans, the assignments, the status and the work are stored in the collaboration database, no matter where I am, I can see what you were supposed to do, what you've done so far and what I'm supposed to do to keep the project going," she says. "I can go right to work and be productive, even if you're asleep and can't show me what you've done. That's a basic principle of our follow-the-sun engineering technique. We've created a whole office without buildings, and without restrictions from geography, corporate boundaries or time zones! That's worth real money to our operation, especially for a company that does outsourced project work without having to put an entire team on site."

IMT also uses a few other tools to help its employees work together no matter where they are, Li says. One is the Web cam. Once in a while, an engineer needs to see the parts that came off the line or the operation of the line itself. Sending the part overnight is an option, but that takes a day. When there's not enough time to do that, a team member can transmit a live video of exactly what is happening via Web cam. It's almost like being in a factory or an operating room watching people do their job.

Another important tool is instant messenger. Since team members are in different cities, it's not possible to have the kind of impromptu chat traditional team members might have in the halls or by stopping by each other's offices. Instant messenger allows for that kind of interaction virtually. If colleagues need to talk to another, they can have a short chat on instant messenger. Or if it's a longer conversation, they can pick up the phone and call.

"Don't you need to see body language?" Ray asks.

"Sometimes, sure, but remember that for the most part, this is engineering, not a negotiation. Besides, you can use your other senses. If people start to get quiet, you know they are troubled or thinking. If they get passionate, you can hear it in their voices. After you begin to get used to it, you learn that you don't need body language to read people's moods," Li says. "You just need to trust your other senses."

"That makes sense," Ray says thoughtfully. "But if you aren't working in the same place, how do you know that people are really at work? Maybe they didn't come in today. Or maybe they are logged on but playing computer games or cruising the Internet."

Li points out that just because people are in the office, that doesn't mean that they are working on what you need them to do. She reminds Ray that these are dedicated and talented product managers and engineers. The best way to get them to work hard is to give them an interesting and challenging assignment with a deadline. Besides, with the collaboration environment, the project manager can tell if the work is being done. The team members status their tasks and store their deliverables where everyone else on the team can see them.

When someone falls behind, she adds, it is usually for a reason other than effort. For example, sometimes the work doesn't get done because a person is struggling with an assignment, so he or she sets up a problem-solving thread using the project collaboration software. This allows other team members to make suggestions and help the person with his or her problems. Or they set up an instant meeting and conduct a problem-solving walk-through. It doesn't always work, Li admits. Some people just need to be in an office with the other members of their team. Some managers can't get used to managing people who are not within 50 feet of their desk.

When that happens, it quickly becomes clear that this isn't right for them, and they go find another place to work, she says. There are plenty of companies where you can commute to an office every day. The people at IMT are very bright. They have no trouble moving on if they don't fit with the culture. Li suggests that at Ray's company, he might want to start with a few select teams that can set the path for those who are more resistant and like the way things have always been done. When the majority begins to get it, he might simply have to let the last of the holdouts leave the company, just as IMT does.

Employees at IMT do travel every once in a while, Li tells Ray. Every few months, IMT brings everyone together in one place to brainstorm about the business, come up with great new ideas, drink some good wine and get to know each other in person.

"But," she continues, "the bottom line is that my office isn't a desk, a filing cabinet and an assistant outside playing gatekeeper. My office is my laptop computer, meeting center software, project collaboration software and instant messenger. I do have an assistant, and he uses the same tools to keep me organized. I can look up anything in the company database from anywhere in the world. I can meet with an employee or a customer from any office or hotel room. All I need is a phone line and an Internet connection. I do keep a nice office at the plant in Jakarta and an office in London to entertain customers and humor investors who like to see people sitting near bricks and mortar. But if they wanted to see the engineering department, I'd need to rent a building and hire actors."

Ray seems a little more convinced. "Give me an example of how this all comes together to make money and why it's better than the normal way of running a business," he says.

"OK, here's one example," Li responds. "Tom Peters once said that a turned-on team isn't 10 to 20 percent more effective but 10 to 500 percent more effective. In our business, we believe that innovation comes wherever you find it." Li tells Ray about Mary, one of IMT's European engineers.

Mary works a very untraditional schedule. She puts in five or six hours during the day when her kids are in school, then another two to three hours in the evening after they go to bed. It works really well because she can work with the team in Europe during the day and a team in the U.S. in the evenings. One day while her kids were in school, she went down to the coffee house near the university and worked from there. With the coffee house's Internet connection and a headset on her cell phone, she was good to go. She had just hung up from a design meeting when she overheard two young engineering graduate students talking about their thesis project. It sounded like a great product idea. So she sent Li an instant message. Mary called Li, and introduced her to the students.

The next day, one of IMT's product managers, who lives a few hours away, met with the students and their supervising professor. IMT made them a fair offer for their idea and worked it out with the university patent office. The young engineers were so excited to learn that Mary lives in town and frequently works from a coffee house that IMT was able to hire these two students—who graduated third and sixth in their graduate school class, Li adds proudly—before they even began looking for jobs.

IMT immediately began design on the product. About a third of the way into proof of concept, a marketing team and a design-for-manufacturing team were assigned. All of the teams ran their projects on the project collaboration database and had regular walk-throughs using the meeting center software to stay coordinated. When design got ahead of schedule by a month, marketing knew about it instantly and adjusted its work accordingly. The marketing team had access to all of the engineering information using the collaboration database and made several design suggestions that made the product more versatile. Manufacturing ran its prototyping projects on database, where it also had access to all of the design information, including the current specifications and all of the change control logs.

"Manufacturing ran most of its walk-throughs with engineering using the Internet meeting manager, but when it had some manufacturing problems, it took a Web cam onto the shop floor, hooked up a meeting and resolved design problems right there, without anyone getting on a plane," Li says.

Li sums up the key benefits of IMT's approach.

- We have a fine engineer in Mary. She stays with us, and is one of our most productive and innovative engineers, because she doesn't have to decide between an exciting career and being home with her kids. Having Mary was the key to this whole success story: We got a product we never would have thought about because an engineer with a nontraditional work environment overheard a conversation in a coffee house.

- We closed out the competition because the CEO was instantly accessible to the average engineer, even though I was in Paris at the time.
- We brought a product to market in two-thirds the time and at two-thirds the cost because we were able to use follow-the-sun engineering and run concurrent projects efficiently with engineering, manufacturing, marketing and even sales.
- We gained two new, talented engineers who have already worked on their first product and who will never think that the way we work is unusual.
- We added their professor to our virtual network, and he will bring us product ideas and good engineers in the future. He's also agreed to serve on one of our product advisory panels.

"By the way," Li adds, "this product is already starting to show great promise as next year's revenue growth engine."

"That's quite a story," Ray admits. "But your company grew up this way. How can a traditional company like mine adapt to this way of working?"

"Well," Chris interjects, "now that we have your attention, would this qualify as an example of a company that is making it work? Let's take a closer look at IMT's processes and decide which ones could work for you."

CHAPTER 4 TAKEAWAYS

IMT has built a successful distributed company, in which employees around the world work together effectively using a few key tools: a **project collaboration environment** where everyone working on a project can store essential information; an **Internet meeting manager,** which facilitates electronic meetings during which participants can share and see exactly what is on each other's computer; **Web cams,** for when a video image is needed; and **instant messenger,** which allows for quick, spontaneous interaction between team members.

The current state of Internet collaboration technology enables business practices that let teams function as if they are in one building, even if team members are distributed around the world. By using this technology effectively, companies can reduce cost, speed up time to market and create a highly motivated labor force.

Chapter 5:
Communication & Relationships

Chris starts by highlighting aspects of Li's experience that fit with Marvin's goals for Ray's team: how she operates at lower cost than a traditional model, including recruiting, retention, the cost of labor, the productivity of her work force and the cost of manufacturing; how she brings together product development, marketing, manufacturing and even sales to launch a product for less money, faster and without the coordination problems that can cost months of lost time; and how her distributed teams let her get closer to her customers and to networks that include universities and partners.

"Those all fit with the objectives Marvin has asked you to meet," Chris says. "Is it worth going on with our discussion to talk about how?"

"Sure," Ray says. "I'm still a little skeptical, but if some of these ideas can scale from a company Li's size to a company the size of Alpha Corp.—and my people can learn how to use them without going backward—then they're certainly worth trying."

"OK, so let's talk about a framework for making communication work, how that framework fits into your traditional processes and how those processes will need to change to take advantage of the new state of the possible," says Chris. "Also, one bit of fair notice: Marvin has already studied Li's company."

"Is that a threat?" Ray asks nervously.

"Not at all. It's just important for you to understand that Marvin already believes in the state of the possible. You know, Ray, what it really comes down to is communication, working relationships, trust and the ability to supervise and motivate people. If you can do those things from a distance, then everything else is pretty simple, right?" Chris continues, focusing on the key challenges of managing teams that are working in different places:

- Running successful meetings whether people are together or apart
- Using a project collaboration environment to establish visibility, and to gain trust and lead with that increased visibility
- Assigning work remotely and supervising remote workers

- Deciding when to have electronic meetings and when to travel to work together and solve problems
- Building trust so that people will escalate an issue or a problem when they know about it
- Bringing it all together into a continuous process to save money and time

"If you have good communication and management principles," Chris adds, "then distance can be managed with a few simple tools. If you lack those management principles, then the distance will multiply those problems a hundredfold."

Chris turns his attention to the first point: how to run effective meetings. He and Ray discuss what makes a good meeting—clear goals, the full attention of the participants and effective use of time—and then talk about the pitfalls of meetings where everyone isn't in the same room. Some people might lose interest and read emails, send instant messages or otherwise "drop out" of the meeting, even if they don't actually hang up the phone.

Ray and Chris agree that in a good meeting, people participate and stay engaged. If the meeting leader notices that someone is drifting, he needs to bring that person back into the meeting, even though he might not be able to see that person playing games or reading email. There are a few simple rules for running a good meeting, whether it's a two-person working session or a company-wide meeting. Chris asks Li to hand Ray the following list of six simple rules her company uses to run effective meetings.

1. When two or more people talk for more than 15 minutes about work, that constitutes a meeting.
2. Start meetings with objectives—not just an agenda—so that you know how to determine if meetings are successful. At IMT, the phrase, "This meeting will be successful if..." is uttered at the start of each meeting.
3. Understand what kind of meeting you are having so that you can accurately define what will make it a success. Since IMT does mostly engineering and marketing, employees there have four kinds of meetings:
    - Presentations
    - Walk-throughs
    - Brainstorming sessions
    - Chats

    A meeting with multiple subjects to cover may be a combination of these types of conversations. The materials used to run the meeting and the work product produced during the meeting will be different depending on which type of conversation is occurring.
4. Use the meeting center to make a common set of materials available for all participants to see. This will allow you to keep people focused and to capture written work products from your meeting. Be religious about doing things in writing so that

everyone attending the same meeting reaches the same conclusion.
5. Agree to the length of the meeting beforehand and ask every attendee to stay in the meeting for that duration without doing anything else, such as emailing, having a separate conversation or playing games.
6. Engage members of the meeting frequently to make sure they are still there.

Li explains that at IMT, they teach people these six rules and then use the rules at every meeting until they become second nature. She adds that when she forgets one of the rules, people usually remind her because they want to use their time well.

"Interesting," Ray says. "Some of the rules make a lot of sense, but others don't. For example, the second rule: What's the difference between an agenda and an objective, and why does it matter?"

Chris jumps in to explain that when he started working with remote teams, he found that people blamed bad meetings on the distance when, in fact, the meetings were just bad. So he started suggesting to Li and others that they start every meeting with the phrase, "This meeting will be a success if we accomplish the following." People agree on the topic that they are going to cover—and how to determine that they are done—beforehand. Sample statements are things like:

- "This meeting will be a success if we review the project status; agree in writing on the accomplishments and where we are ahead (and behind) in the plan; discuss the open issues and risks; and agree in writing on corrective actions and assignments of responsibilities."
- "This meeting will be a success if we can review these project deliverables, make changes in writing or sign off on those deliverables."

In both of the above statements, there is a clear definition of success; the result of the meeting is in writing and people can tell during the meeting whether they are accomplishing the task at hand. At various points in the meeting, they can stop and ask, "Are we being successful?" Contrast that with a meeting whose agenda says:

- "Discuss project status."
- "Discuss project deliverables."

The second meeting might be successful, Chris says, but it is up to the meeting leader to get people focused. If people have different definitions of the importance of the meeting and its outcome, then they hijack the meeting to their own purposes—or drop out entirely because they don't agree that the meeting is an important use of their time. Even if everyone is together, that's a hard meeting to run. "When people are apart, it becomes nearly impossible," Chris says.

Chris points out that the conversation he, Li and Ray are having constitutes a meeting. He might define the success of this meeting by saying, "This meeting will be successful if:"

- Ray leaves believing that at least one other company out there is able to use a completely distributed labor force work and get better results than in the past.
- Ray leaves understanding and believing that it is possible to communicate, build trust, supervise and motivate people at a distance as well as if they were in the same location.

"I guess you told me that in advance, didn't you?" Ray laughs.

"Yes we did," Chris agrees. "There were no hidden agendas. We just didn't force you into the rigor of our process because you didn't believe in it yet. But it was there all along."

Li explains how to use the third rule. In every situation, you must know what kind of meeting you are having, she says. A **presentation** is a mostly one-way communication. The purpose is to teach, sell or convince. So the meeting leader might begin this kind of meeting with the statement, "This meeting will be a success if Ray is convinced that this stuff works and he understands the principles and tools." Every once in a while, the leader should stop and ask, "Does this make sense?" says Li. If it does, the leader can go on; if not, he or she can handle questions and objections. The presentation materials and follow-up materials are then stored in the collaboration database.

In a **walk-through**, the meeting leader wants changes or an explicit agreement to a new work product being developed. So, if Chris and Li were writing a book and Ray were their editor, they might ask Ray to read a draft chapter in advance, and then ask him if they had made the right points and gotten them across clearly. They would then come to the meeting with the manuscript, mark up any changes and make a list of things to rework before the next review.

If Chris and Li were designing a product or a marketing campaign instead, then there would be deliverables such as product requirements, designs, feature and benefit discussions and marketing literature. They would have Ray review those deliverables, and if he approved them, store them in the collaboration database and mark the task as complete. If he didn't agree, the team could create an open item list or mark up the deliverable and schedule the rework and next review session. And since they would be working on materials, they could all look at them at the same time with the meeting center software. "Sharing the deliverables with the meeting center keeps everyone focused on the materials and the purpose of the meeting," Li says.

The next kind of meeting is a **brainstorming session.** In this type of meeting, the participants need to start with a good definition of the problem they are trying to solve, and then advance a number of ideas that can be used to solve the problem. That can be done on a flip chart or a whiteboard. The team can even open a Word document or a PowerPoint presentation where they can create the materials as they work.

The last type of meeting is a **chat**. A chat occurs when two or more people get together and throw out some ideas, build working relationships and think out of the box. No work product is produced, but team members get to know each other's minds. "That's good as well," says Li, "as long as you are not trying to get to an agreement."

"Why not?" Ray asks.

"Because you didn't write it down," Li says. "So how will you ever agree later to what you agreed upon today?"

"So, it's a chat unless we write it down and store it in the collaboration database?" Ray asks.

"Exactly," says Li. She promises Ray they'll take a break soon, but she has a few more points to make. The fifth rule is to agree to the length of the meeting beforehand and ask every member of the team to stay for the entire meeting. But everyone has a saturation point, Li cautions, so people eventually need to stop and absorb what they have heard. "When you reach that point, the meeting leader will want to schedule a break or stop the meeting and start again the next day when everyone is fresh," she says. "Stop when people look like they need a break, and you'll get the same level of intensity every time you gather. Then people won't wander, and you won't have to keep asking them questions to bring them back into the meeting."

"I guess that makes sense," Ray agrees. "But how can you tell when people are drifting out of the meeting if you can't see them?"

"Ah," says Li, "the final point." She highlights a few ways to tell if you've lost someone's attention: If people stop talking or seem quiet, then you can guess that you've lost them. If you haven't heard a person's voice for a while, it is probably a good idea to stop and ask a question that brings the person back into the meeting. If people start answering in monosyllables, that's a sign it's time to stop the meeting and start again on another day. When people who are normally very clear and articulate start to lose their train of thought and not make sense, then they are probably doing something else. Ask them a few questions and bring them back into the meeting, or let them finish what they are doing before you restart.

"Now," Li concludes, smiling broadly, "I'm here to build relationships and brainstorm great ideas. Chris, let's add Ray to our network and meet some friends in the bar for a good bottle of wine."

Chapter 5 Takeaways

The six essential rules for effective meetings are as follows:
1. If two or more people work on something for more than 15 minutes, that constitutes a meeting.
2. Start meetings with objectives, not just agendas.
3. Know what kind of meeting you are having and what work product you should produce.
4. Use an Internet meeting manager for all remote meetings, so that everyone sees the same materials and work products.
5. Agree to the length of the meeting and ask everyone to stay in the meeting until the end.
6. Engage participants regularly so that you keep their minds on the meeting.

There are four types of meetings:
1. Presentation: Generally one-sided, this type of meeting is designed to teach, present or convince.
2. Walk-through: This type of meeting is designed to work out changes or obtain agreement on a product.
3. Brainstorming session: The purpose of this kind of meeting is to generate ideas with other team members.
4. Chat: The purpose of chats is to get to know other team members and share thoughts informally.

CHAPTER 6:

GUIDING PRINCIPLES

The next morning over breakfast, Ray, Chris and Li gather again. Ray greets Chris and Li warmly. "Well, that was some great wine and some really interesting people. How do you know them?"

Chris laughs and explains that Li has an unfair advantage when it comes to running remote teams. Many years ago, he tells Ray, he and some others started a global school of very bright students and had them attend school daily, using the same tools and techniques they are showing Ray. They studied the children as they developed, and many of their principles evolved from that. The kids started getting together occasionally for summer vacations and other breaks. Pretty soon that turned into an annual gathering, and it has increased by a few people every year as members bring new people into the network.

"We'll tell you a bit more about that and how it applies to your company later," Chris says, "but first let's pick up just a few more points. Then we'll have all the basic principles in place. Yesterday we talked a lot about meetings because they are the basis of how we communicate verbally and how we reach agreements. In every verbal meeting, we create written work products so that the team has records of the decisions they make and the ideas they create. Now, here are a few things we'll talk about today:"

- How to run successful meetings whether you are together or apart—and how that becomes especially important when you are apart
- How to use the project collaboration environment to establish visibility and how to lead by using that increased visibility
- How to take time out of problem-solving by using escalation versus blame-setting to solve problems and by having problem-solving meetings immediately rather than waiting until everyone can get together
- How to assign and supervise projects with remote workers
- When to have electronic meetings and when to travel to work together and solve problems
- How it all comes together in a continuous process to save time and money

"So, today, let's talk briefly about the rest of the principles," says Chris. "We'll start with collaboration environments."

Li jumps in to point out that while they've talked a lot about deliverables, they haven't talked about the overall project process and what's needed in a project environment. She lists some essential requirements.

1. You need to know what projects you should really work on, so that you don't waste time and top talent on unimportant projects.
2. For each project, you need a definition of scope and a plan that is visible to every member of the team. That way, all team members know what they are supposed to work on and how that work fits within the whole project.
3. You need a place to store the deliverables, or the work products, and a place to keep track of the status of each piece of the work.
4. As project members find issues and identify risks, they need a place to write them down and a way to record how they are going to be resolved.
5. As an executive, you need a quick way to see the status of all of the projects that are important to you and a way to resolve problems quickly.

Li explains that waste occurs when project managers or team leaders don't have a clear picture of what the organization wants from them, when managers fail to communicate those goals to team members or when the scope of a project changes part way through. Meanwhile, time gets wasted, and work gets done that has to be changed, repeated or thrown away.

When you spread that team out over 12 time zones and 9,000 miles, it's a lot harder to just walk down the hall and solve a problem, Li says. A project collaboration environment creates structure around the information. It lets people know what they are supposed to do, and it quickly identifies the problems that need to be solved and the impact of not solving them. Once an issue gets resolved, all of the team members know the solution, and weeks later they can go back and look it up again. People are more productive because they know what's expected from them. Plus, fewer things get done twice, and less time gets wasted waiting for someone to solve a problem.

Chris breaks in to point out how Ray can use these tools to integrate acquired teams into his product development system. He can then use them to integrate manufacturing, marketing, sales and product development to get better and faster product launches. Teams from multiple sites can work on the same problem with the exact same fact base, decide what to do and update the project collaboration database with the same information.

The next step is to get people to tell you the truth in the collaboration environment, Li says. Ray looks indignant at first, but Li explains that this is not a reflection of Ray's team, but simply human nature: People will report positive progress and hide problems, hoping they can solve them rather than bring them to a manager's attention. Yet managers want to know about problems early on so they can leverage the right resources to help find a solution. "That is the essential tension that exists in every organization," says Li.

Chris offers a well-known example from the early experience of the Saturn manufacturing lines: Any worker could stop the line to report or fix a problem, but everyone was afraid to be the first person to pull the stop cord.

The hardest part is getting people to understand that visibility is a good thing, Chris says. Reporting problems early and allowing the best minds to work on them is critical. Rewarding visibility must come from the top; otherwise, you will have a well-structured set of partial information, and the real escalations and communications of the truth will go on in the back channels of the office. Managing with visibility requires escalating early with the facts, instead of placing blame later when nothing can be done. Most organizations need to get people to escalate too much, then they can scale back to just the things that need visibility. Getting a balance, in which the right escalations get to the right people at the right time, is the key to making this work.

"I think I'm getting it," Rays says. "These are the same basic principles we try to teach all of the time. You're just talking about creating visibility and making communication second nature within the organization's headquarters and across remote teams. That seems like something I can do, but what about supervising employees at a distance? That seems more challenging."

Li walks Ray through the simple process for assigning and supervising work that she uses at IMT.

1. Plan the work all the way down to the task level in the project collaboration environment.
2. Conduct an assignment walk-through between the manager and the person performing the work to make sure that the person doing the work understands the requirement and the deliverable he or she is to produce. IMT managers frequently go back to the phrase, "This task will be successful if we accomplish the following."
3. As work proceeds, you may or may not need to conduct problem-solving walk-throughs to make sure that the person is not confused or stuck. This really requires trust and judgment between the manager and the employee.
4. As work progresses, store the work in the project collaboration environment, where people can access it and where the manager can periodically review it with the employee.
5. Conduct a walk-through when the work is complete to get sign-off from the sponsor and the manager before the person goes on to the next assignment.

Of course, there are always times when someone has a problem and the person he or she needs to talk to isn't at work or is in another time zone, says Li. Often, the answers are in the project collaboration environment, because the documentation and deliverables are all right there. If that doesn't work, then the person can schedule time for a problem-solving walk-through and work on something else until that happens. Little time losses like that can be overcome, and the advantages of a distributed team far outweigh the disadvantages.

"People just need to get used to a slightly different way of thinking," Li says. "The techniques that managers use to supervise are the same as they have always been. Everyone just needs to be a little more disciplined."

CHAPTER 6 TAKEAWAYS

Here are some key steps in assigning work and supervising employees remotely:

- Use the project collaboration environment to create visibility so employees know what they are to work on and everyone on the team can see both the project status and the project work product.
- Escalation is critical to take time out of problem solving. Use the project collaboration environment to identify issues early on and get team and executive involvement to resolve problems before they impact the team's productivity.
- Assigning and supervising work is one of the things that changes most in the distributed world. The Internet meeting manager allows supervisors to conduct assignment walk-throughs and task completion reviews, the same as if the team were in one place. It's also a quick way to solve problems as they occur.

Chapter 7: Business Travel

Ray looks thoughtful. "I think I'm beginning to believe the possibilities, and I can see how this might work for me. It seems to me, though, that no matter how well the system works, you still need to travel every once in a while."

"Exactly," Li says, nodding. "We find that when people get to know each other, they trust each other more. That has given us a lot of insight into what to do in meetings when we do get together versus meetings we have electronically via the meeting center."

Traditional companies often think that when you are bringing people together for a meeting, you should work very hard and get a lot done, Li explains. They tend to run from eight in the morning until six or even eight at night and cover so much material that by the end of the first day, people are exhausted, and they are only absorbing a small part of the material.

"At IMT, we use physical meetings and gatherings to build friendships and trust and to work on things that are really hard to do in remote meetings," Li says. "Then, when we do our regular work, we know one another better, we can read each other better and we understand more about each other's feelings. We can even use funny episodes from our time together to relieve the tension when we disagree passionately about something."

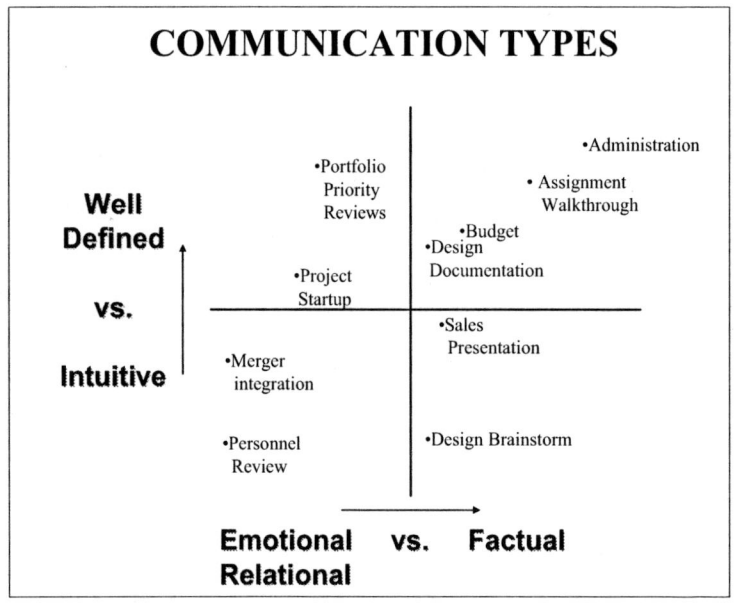

Chris hands a diagram to Ray. "This picture helps us decide when to gather and when to work electronically. The things that plot as very factual and well-defined lend themselves well to remote meetings.

Things that plot as more intuitive and emotional or relationship-oriented tend to require us to get together in one place. The longer we work together, the further we can stretch the things we can do without getting together, which makes us faster and cheaper."

Li mentions that the gathering they attended the previous night is a great example of when it is important to be together. She and Chris have formed a very unique network of people with a common view of how to run global companies. They work together regularly but gather once a year to meet and renew friendships and working relationships. At IMT, working teams get together at least two or three times a year to build the sense of team. The whole company gets together once a year for the same reason. "Those meetings have a pretty soft agenda for content and a rich agenda for brainstorming and relationship building," Li says.

"There are other reasons to travel, and you have to evaluate each on its own merit," Chris adds. "Team kickoff meetings, major brainstorming sessions and working out inter-team arguments are all good reasons to travel, and they might make your team a lot more productive in the long run. Preparing and walking through materials, design meetings, budgeting and financial planning are all better done with meeting software, so that the deliverables are stored in the collaboration environment where everyone can find them."

Chris reminds Ray that there's no reason to do any of this if it doesn't save money. By running a distributed environment, you can take employees from anywhere, put them on a team and make them fully productive as part of that team. You can solve any problem when it occurs.

"Now contrast that to the way work often happens," Chris says, as he hands a chart to Ray. "People find a problem that is too difficult to solve with faxes, telephone calls and emails, so they schedule a meeting, fly to get in one room and solve the problem. They think that it is expensive because of the cost and time of travel, but that is just the tip of the iceberg. The real loss is wasted productivity and lost time on the project as you try to get everyone to compare calendars, schedule a time when everyone can travel and then wait for the meeting."

Instead, it's better to document the issue in the collaborative database where everyone can see it and assign it to the team that needs to do the work, Chris explains. You use the meeting manager software to call an immediate meeting and discuss the issue, agree to the problem and perhaps brainstorm alternative solutions. As work proceeds, you conduct regular walk-throughs to get buy-in. By the time you could have gotten everyone in the same room, you have solved the problem and moved on—at a fraction of the cost, a fraction of the delay to the project and a fraction of the impact on your professional lives.

"OK, OK, I've got it," Ray says, smiling. "But it doesn't look easy. How do I change my company from the way we've always done things? Li, you built your company this way, so it's second nature for you. Assuming that we can make this work, how much will it disrupt us while we change, how long will it take and how much will it cost?"

Chris responds, "Ray, the changes can be gradual over a year or longer. Take the parts of your company that will benefit the most first, and then make them the pilots and examples for everyone else. One day you will look up and, like Li, it will just be the way things are done."

"Well, Ray," Li says, "I think we've covered a lot of ground. I'm going to head out now to spend time with my friends and business associates, but remember that we are now members of a virtual network. As you and Chris work through the changes to your company, we can talk anytime you like. I'll send you my instant messenger address so that you can find me anytime. Maybe we can even find some ways to make money together as you continue to build your company's remote teams. It's been great to meet you."

"Thank you, Li. I must admit that after our conversation, I believe that your methods could help my company. We'll see where we go from here."

Chapter 7 Takeaways

In day-to-day work, companies can save a great deal of time and money by using an Internet meeting manager to meet remotely. However, gathering distributed teams together in one place can be very effective for certain types of meetings, such as:

- Team kick-off meetings
- Major brainstorming sessions
- Working out inter-team arguments
- Getting to know each other

Chapter 8: Getting Started

A few days later, Chris meets with Sandra and Ray to begin the process of implementing the "being there" methods for Ray's teams. Chris begins by explaining a few simple steps and principles. "Remember, people love progress, but they hate change," he says. He reminds Sandra and Ray that word processing, email and the Internet were all rejected by established leaders until it became apparent that they were essential in staying competitive. He explains that they should begin with the assumption that there will be holdouts and that making these changes will require a lot of effort. The leaders of the changes must be top management: They need to learn and use the technologies, but more important, they must lead others in new ways of thinking about how to run the business. Chris points out that they're already doing three things right:

- Marvin is a highly visible supporter of these changes, and he has established measurable business improvements that he wants to see as a result. He has given this the priority that it needs and provided a way to measure its success.
- Ray has put Sandra in charge and given her the time and the resources to implement these changes. That is a tremendous commitment, one that will be visible to people who might assume this is just another new business idea that will go away if they ignore it long enough.
- Ray has learned enough about the possibilities that he believes this can be successful, so people won't keep waiting for a signal from him as to whether they should get on board. On the other hand, Chris still senses a glimmer of doubt when it comes to managing remote team members. Ray needs to suppress that doubt and believe that this is going to work, or people will sense his skepticism.

"Well, Chris," Ray responds, "I see examples of where it works, but it still cuts across a lot of the principles that I've grown up with. I believe in it, but it's still a tremendous leap of faith. But I'll take that leap and demonstrate my confidence in it so the team buys in."

Chris smiles, pleased at Ray's response. He launches in to the four key questions to consider before implementing the "being there without going there" methods:

GETTING STARTED

- What are the spheres of influence of the organization and the steps and sponsors Ray will need as he expands from the departments he controls to his peer organizations, then to the extended enterprise and ultimately to a virtual labor force?
- What is the organization's level of readiness to accept new processes?
- What steps does Ray need to take to make this work for each group that he brings on board?
- How will Ray achieve the benefits, and how will he drive those benefits to real economic value that he can describe to the board of directors?

Spheres of Influence

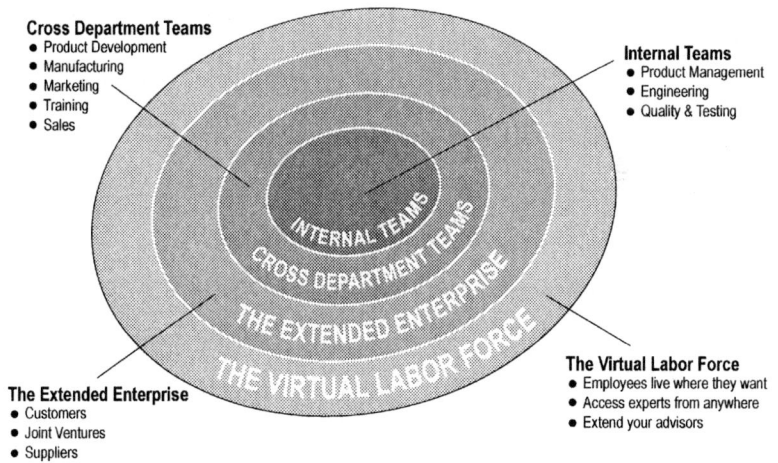

Cross Department Teams
- Product Development
- Manufacturing
- Marketing
- Training
- Sales

Internal Teams
- Product Management
- Engineering
- Quality & Testing

The Extended Enterprise
- Customers
- Joint Ventures
- Suppliers
- Merger Candidates
- Consultants
- Offshore Development

The Virtual Labor Force
- Employees live where they want
- Access experts from anywhere
- Extend your advisors

"Let's start with the spheres that you will need to influence to get the effect you are reaching for." Chris slides a chart across the table with four concentric circles. Each circle represents an extension of the enterprise where Chris' methods produce real economic value.

- The inside circle is Ray's product development organization, comprised of product managers and engineers. They have similar disciplines and are all within a single organization. They have well-defined methods, so they are focused on adding a few new principles and processes around the distributed enterprise.
- The second ring represents the organizations within the company that span marketing, production and other disciplines, all with varying methods and varying attention to concepts like project management. As you begin to seriously cross organizational boundaries, you introduce politics. Who do these cross-discipline teams report to? Who is really in charge of a product launch? The methods are the same, but they require you to think of things as a program rather than a project. They also require people who don't think like project members to learn some new ways of thinking. Finally, it requires a powerful sponsor to get people to play on a single team.
- The third ring is where these methods begin to cross beyond traditional corporate boundaries to work more directly with customers, suppliers, joint ventures, consultants and

contractors. From a technology perspective, this ring introduces firewalls and a variety of issues about sharing information while retaining security. From a behavioral perspective, it requires people to extend trust across these boundaries, share information and operate on facts rather than emotions and personal agendas. It also requires some substantial effort when people begin to think about working around the 24-hour clock and working with teams in places such as India.

- The fourth ring brings everything full circle. By the time you're working across all of these boundaries, you are a black belt at distributed management. People can begin to live and work anywhere they want, and you will become expert at judging results, not attendance and effort. You can create high-performance teams that don't live in the same place. You can reduce turnover to less than 5 percent, assuming you are hiring the right people in the first place.

Sandra jumps in. "Ray, the team thinks we should start in the first ring, focusing primarily on our sphere of influence, with just a few related players, such as marketing and a few contractors, coming in from the second ring. That way we can get our disciplines right and get the first wave of economic value. Then, as we present it to our peers and people outside the company, we can point to well-documented solutions and well-documented value."

"Right," says Chris. "But remember that each ring has to buy into the processes, so if you can get some of their champions to observe and make suggestions in your first project, then as this gets to them, it will be easier to accept because they had a role in creating it."

12 Easy Steps

Chris explains the steps for execution. He suggests that Sandra and Ray repeat these steps with each new team that is brought into this approach.

1. Acquire the three basic technologies that are going to be the baseline for making this work—instant messenger, a project collaboration database and an Internet meeting manager. Web cams and electronic whiteboards can be added after people get used to the basics.
2. Find a core group of advocates who are innovative and challenged by change. They must be managers, thought leaders and experts that others respect.
3. Train these advocates on the technology and discuss the state of the possible for the business.
4. Document the business values that you are going to get from the change and how you will measure those values. This is an important step because you will occasionally lose your resolve, and the measurable values will strengthen that resolve and get you back on track.
5. Create a simple document of the business process changes that you will make to achieve the business values. This will include

everything from periodic management meetings spanning multiple locations to managing product development deliverables and information.

6. Pick a set of meaningful projects that will let you learn the technologies and changes in business practices, but will also let you adjust your business practices until they are simple, easy to remember and able to produce the values that you desire.
7. Train people on both the technologies and the business practices at the same time. Start small, so that each step produces an immediately noticeable value to the participants, but with a minimum of difficulty. Each time a step is made, add another level of complexity. Walk, then run; and finally, fly.
8. Execute your programs with the new procedures.
9. Measure your results and adjust your processes.
10. Expand the number of people and programs that have embraced the changes, always measuring and adjusting your processes.
11. Expand your processes and technologies, adding tools like Web cams and electronic whiteboards and embracing changes like brainstorming without getting on airplanes.
12. Learn the limits of where you get diminishing returns and stop there. Then, every once in a while ask if it is time to stretch a boundary. It is better to go slow, and find out you could have gone faster, than to risk disillusioning your teams because you pushed the learning curve to fast for them to keep up. Children take months learning to crawl, then to walk and then to run. This, too, will take time.

"That seems like a lot of steps," Sandra says. "How long does it take to get started, and how long does it take to begin to produce the kind of value that will meet Marvin's goals?"

Critical Success Factors

"Those are good questions," replies Chris. "There are several variables that are going to affect the timeline."

1. Do you have documented processes now, and will they lend themselves well to the approach that we are discussing? Tribal knowledge, processes and skills passed on to new team members, verbally and through exposure, are far more difficult to work with. Those processes will need to be documented early on.
2. Can you absorb the impact of this change in your business? It will take an investment of time as well as money and will not yield immediate payback until you learn to embrace the new way of doing things and do it consistently.
3. Are your people receptive to change and willing to believe in the state of the possible? Beware the contrary argument of, "This is the way we have always done things." This is simply not true. If it were, we'd still be sitting in caves, drawing on the walls, using a torch for light. Help people to understand that change is inevitable, and that managing and embracing change will make it valuable instead of painful.

4. Do you have the top-down commitment to work through problems and to demonstrate that this is a lasting change to the company, not an experiment that might fail? If you succeed, and your competitor does not, you stand to take his entire share of the market by bringing superior products to the market faster and cheaper.

Chris adds that he thinks Ray and Sandra currently have good processes and a core group of people who are fairly receptive to change. If their company's leaders accept this plan, he expects they will begin to see results in three to four months and will notice a remarkable change within a year. Chris believes they can meet Marvin's goals—though he warns them Marvin will probably be impatient. He explains that they are killing a lot of sacred cows, and it takes people a while to get used to that. Intellectually, Marvin understands that, but he has little patience for people who stonewall good ideas.

Measuring Success

Chris moves on. "Now let's talk about your business, the business values we are reaching for and the processes that we must change to get them. But first, let's discuss the difference between a benefit and a value and set some fairly rigorous definitions for a value."

A **benefit** is an improvement that is good for the business. Examples are increased visibility, faster decision-making, better decision-making based on facts, better team morale and improved customer satisfaction. A **value** must pass a higher standard. It's a measurable improvement in the business that can be quantified and converted to a dollar value. So a value must either increase revenue or decrease expense. Chris suggests that they place four conditions on a value:

- It must be measurable. For example: "We will decrease project costs by 5 percent by eliminating rework with increased visibility and quicker problem-solving."
- It must be an important amount: 1 to 2 percent improvement in all projects may be enough to cover the cost of the technology and the change, but it will not be enough to keep management's attention when other demands impose themselves. And it will not be important enough to work through the rough spots of change.
- It must be actionable. For example: "We will measurably reduce the hard dollar cost of contractors and travel on our five biggest projects" or "We will reduce head count by not filling open positions" or "We will increase revenue by 8 percent by reducing time to market for two major product releases."
- It must be palatable. If you have just reduced head count by 15 percent, an improvement in productivity is only palatable if you can get more done and increase revenue. It is probably not palatable to go through another reduction in head count to pay for this set of technology

and business changes. Increase productivity by avoiding the time delays that occur when you have to travel for emergencies. Then, instead of reducing head count again, use the cost savings from the travel events that you have avoided.

"The good news is that Marvin has given us a set of measurable goals that meet almost all of the definitions above," says Sandra. "Chris and I have come up with the following list of opportunities to explore with our champions."

- Reduce cost by 6 to 10 percent over the course of a year. Immediate opportunities include contractors, travel, recruiting costs, lower cost per head through use of offshore software development and elimination of head count through normal attrition. Marvin offered to help with the rest of the cost savings by cutting unnecessary programs through better portfolio management. The team will need to hold him to that in order to get the total 10 to 12 percent that he wants for next year.
- Improve cycle time by 90 days, or 20 percent, for new product releases. Marvin slipped a little on this one because he didn't monetize it, Sandra says. If we get products out 20 percent faster, will it necessarily be cheaper or generate more revenue? Sandra says that while they'll need to explore that question, she thinks they can expect a material reduction in cost in product development. The real payoff is in starting the revenue flow

from new products 90 days sooner, with the supply chain, marketing and sales fully up to speed with each launch. Those changes can be documented for each product using some of the data from past launches.

- Improve customer intimacy by having more interaction between engineering and the customers during the design cycle. They know how to achieve the objective, but need to work with marketing and sales to be sure they convert that customer satisfaction to higher revenue per existing account or lower cost of sale in new accounts.
- Integrate four new acquisitions into product development. Some ideas for cost savings here are reduced travel during integration, higher retention of key staff and lower replacement and recruiting costs. The team should also be able to drive product integration much faster, resulting in substantial increases in revenue that can be built into the acquisition business cases.

"Well, Sandra, you've given this a lot of thought," Ray says. "Are you comfortable committing to those goals?"

"Not yet," she replies. "We haven't done the work to quantify the values yet. But we can certainly see the possibilities, and a number of your direct reports have started volunteering places where they could make money if we can make this work. We think that the above list is an excellent hypothesis to prove as we do the work in the next few weeks."

"That's excellent. Marvin will be pleased with our progress. Can you and Chris come to my weekly meeting with him this afternoon?" Ray asks.

"Of course," Sandra says, handing a second list to Ray. "One more thing: We've met with your direct reports, and these are the processes we think we need to change to make this work as we go through the basic concentric circles. We'll revise and work with this list a lot over the next year or two."

Basic Project Skills
1. Project planning and portfolio reporting: The company needs to better define projects of all sizes. It does that pretty well for the large ones, but a lot of time is wasted on smaller ones.
2. Project staffing: Design a process to help managers become aware of the skills of people at other locations, and hold a staffing meeting to agree on the best use of resources.
3. Project startup, brainstorming and execution: Decide how much can be done without traveling and when to bring the team into one place.
4. Assigning work to and supervising people at remote sites: Make sure everyone understands the expectations involved in working with remote teams.

Managing Across Boundaries

5. Manage product launch: Determine how best to manage programs that cut across organizations and geographies so that all of the departments are on a single page and avoid the slips that occurred in the last few launches.
6. Continuous interaction with the factory: Develop processes the factory can use to keep in touch with all of the engineering teams, in order to reduce time and cost in the testing and problem-solving cycles.
7. Solve problems with new products at the customer site: Set up procedures to solve problems the moment they arise.

Managing Across Corporate Boundaries

8. Interact with customers: Bring talent to bear at the customer site from anywhere in the world.
9. Run joint venture teams: Put in place methods for working more effectively with suppliers.
10. Make offshore software development work: Leverage the 24-hour clock and reduce cost by 50 to60 percent for work done offshore.

Hiring and Retaining Talent

11. Hire and motivate remote workers.
12. Provide flexibility and alternative lifestyles for the labor force to increase retention of key talent.

"If we can do these things, then we're confident we can reduce cost, shorten product cycles and agree with sales on how to leverage engineering to drive better revenue," Sandra says. "We should easily achieve Marvin's objectives, with the first benefits beginning to accrue in three to four months."

CHAPTER 8 TAKEAWAYS

Here's a brief version of Chris and Sandra's 12-step guide to execution. These strategies can be applied to almost any company:

1. Acquire the basic technologies required to run distributed teams.
2. Find a core group of advocates.
3. Train these advocates on the technology and discuss the state of the possible for the business.
4. Document the business values that you want to achieve and how you will measure those values.
5. Document the business process changes that you will make to achieve those values.
6. Pick a set of meaningful projects that will allow you to learn the technologies and changes in business practices.
7. Train people on the technologies and the business practices.
8. Execute your programs with the new procedures.
9. Measure your results and adjust your processes.
10. Expand the number of people and programs that have embraced the changes.
11. Expand your processes and technologies.
12. Take care to learn the limits of where you get diminishing returns. Then hold steady until the organization has absorbed the changes and is ready to move forward again.

Chapter 9:

The Home Court First

A month later, Sandra, Chris and their project team give Ray the first full status report. Sandra opens the status booklet from the project collaboration environment and begins by saying that this meeting will be a success if they:

- Review the project plan and the current status against the 12-step process that Chris outlined at the last meeting.
- Get Ray's approval on the list of advocates they have selected to lead the change in the division.
- Get Ray's feedback and approval on the business values they have targeted to achieve in the first phase of the implementation.
- Get Ray's feedback on the business practices that the team feels must change.

- Get Ray's approval on the target projects they plan to use to validate the business practice changes.

Sandra continues, explaining that she and her team set out to work through the first 10 steps of the 12-step process over a three-month period. They are now at the end of the first month. So far, they have accomplished the first three steps (acquiring the technologies, selecting a group of advocates and training those advocates) and are close to documenting the business values and business practices. They have a list of projects in which they plan to pilot the new processes before rolling the program out to the rest of the product managers. They hope to gain broad acceptance of these changes across the entire division over the next three months for a total six-month implementation period. They also plan to have the business values and business practices ready in another six weeks and to be fully into the 10-project pilot three months from the beginning of this initiative.

"That's outstanding, Sandra!" Ray responds. "I spoke with Marvin late last week, and he is delighted with the progress we're making and the results that we anticipate. We'll brief him monthly once we get fully into the implementation."

Sandra looks pleased. She outlines the four topics they need to address in today's meeting:
- Advocates
- Target business values

- Processes to change within the product development cycle during the first phase of implementation
- Pilot projects

Advocates and the Core Technologies

"We were surprised at the number of leaders who wanted to be advocates for the change," Sandra says. There were three particularly compelling reasons that people gave for wanting to be lead a pilot for the program:

- Dave has teams here at headquarters and at the other engineering campus, and he works extensively with the marketing teams in Europe. He feels that if people embraced these changes, he could cut his personal travel by 25 percent and reduce the cost and elapsed time of his projects.
- Mary has a high-priority program, and she knows that we do not have all of the talent that she needs at this campus. She feels the program would help her get the specialized talent she needs from a group that exists in the London center.
- Bob works at the London campus and thinks this program would help him get the visibility he needs within the company without moving his family to the headquarters campus here in Detroit. Bob was here as part of the kickoff, but from now on, he will be attending status meetings using the meeting center software and a conference phone.

All of them are excited about the possibility of being part of a program that has Marvin's sponsorship to produce major improvements in the core products of the company. With this core group of aggressive thought leaders, the team believes that all of the pilot projects and the people who will work on the business processes can come from their areas. Sandra will also use the advocates to pre-sell these ideas to peers in marketing, manufacturing and sales, as well as to some of the joint venture partners, so there will be early acceptance of these concepts when they get ready to work across divisional and corporate boundaries.

Chris' team helped Sandra do a rapid selection of the technologies. Instant messenger is widely available and free, so they simply chose one version. They were also able to find vendors that would host a project collaboration environment and an Internet meeting manager. Since they didn't have to install the tools in their own data center, they were able to accelerate the project and get the advocates trained quickly. All of the technology is installed and ready to use as they go through the business process design and begin the core training programs.

"I think we can mark this phase of the project complete, if that is acceptable to you," Sandra concludes.

Ray responds, "I have a couple of questions. First, that seems very fast for product selection and installation. Have you built consensus within the division and the other teams around the products selected? Also, some of the product information that we are going to be working with is very confidential. Are you comfortable that using hosted services is an adequate way for us to protect our core information?"

"Good questions," Sandra says. Two of the products (the meeting manager and instant messenger) are fairly easy to swap out and replace. She admits they sacrificed some consensus-building for speed, but feels comfortable that they could change to a different solution. The project collaboration database is more complex to change, but they found a market-leading product and are using it to support the next eight weeks of the business redesign. With Chris' recommendation, she's confident that it's a strong product that they can build consensus around during the business process design and pilot. Still, if it ends up being the wrong product, they can swap it out in the next four months with relatively little cost and disruption.

Sandra also explains that she addressed the security issue with the vendors and looked at security evaluations that had been done by their other customers. Since they will eventually be working across corporate boundaries, they opted to put the hosted environment outside the company's firewall. This way, when they add customers, joint venture partners and contractors into the mix, they'll have the ability to protect the information while not penetrating that firewall. "This setup makes the information technology group more comfortable than letting outsiders inside the corporate firewall," she says.

"OK," Ray says, "let's mark this phase complete and go on. But let's make sure we get the consensus we need over the next two months, and let's have our security experts confirm the security evaluations."

Measurable Business Values

Next, Sandra addresses measurable business values. She put Marvin's four main challenges in front of the group:

- Reduce the total cost of product development by 10 to 12 percent.
- Improve revenue by using the product management group to get closer to major customers.
- Reduce the average product release cycle from 15 months to 12 months.
- Be ready to take on four acquisitions in the next year and integrate those teams without relocation.

Sandra thinks they already have a good start on two of the points within the organization. The other two challenges have a major effect on other groups and will be addressed in later phases of the project. The team can see how to achieve a substantial improvement in cost and how to work more closely with the customers. They can also make some improvements in the product release cycle, but the biggest gains will come through extending these tools and techniques to work more closely with peers in marketing, sales, manufacturing and logistics. The biggest time losses in the product launch cycles are in the coordination and handoffs between groups. Those issues will be addressed in the second phase of the implementation. For now, though, the team has looked only at those things that fall within Ray's division and think it's possible to improve product development cycles by close to a month.

Sandra lists some opportunities she and the team see to reduce costs:

- Contractors can be eliminated through more effective use of existing employees.
- Salaries for some open positions can be left empty if they can improve efficiency enough to do the work without those hires. Recruiting costs for those positions will then be zero.
- Attrition can also be used to reduce headcount for a few current positions that will not be filled because of efficiencies that can be gained through these techniques.
- Temporary and permanent relocation costs and travel costs between locations can be reduced.
- Recruiting costs and lost productivity that might have otherwise been incurred due to an employee leaving because of lifestyle reasons can be reduced.

She turns the page to a spreadsheet and says, "Some simple math says we can save at least 5 percent without any direct cutbacks in headcount, by making better use of our people and our travel and relocation budgets and by letting attrition take care of the rest. We've gotten to this point in the process believing that we can get an important hard-dollar savings that is actionable and palatable. We aren't cutting any sacred programs or laying off any employees. Is that a good start on the 10 to 15 percent cost savings that Marvin wants from the division?"

"I would say that's an excellent start," Ray says. "Two questions: First, can we track and demonstrate the improvements within a 12-month window? Second, have the rest of our leaders signed off on your arithmetic and the actions that we have to take?"

"We can achieve the payback in 12 months as long as we haven't double-counted any employees in other programs," Sandra responds. "We're verifying that we aren't double-counting, and we've set up the expected costs in the collaboration system with the target dates so that we take the actions necessary to achieve the improvements and track our progress. We are getting final sign-off on the savings from the group heads now; we may need you to twist an arm or two to get commitments, but we are confident that they are attainable."

"OK, let's put that on this week's management agenda, and we'll get the sign-off recorded," Ray says.

Sandra looks relieved. "Good. Also, we found that product development is usually about 12 months of the 15-month development cycle. We have recorded the intent to reduce the product development cycle by about one month within the division. That means we will need to get the other two months out of the development cycle by working more effectively with the other divisions. Is that sufficient?"

"Yes," says Ray.

Chapter 9 Takeaways

Sandra gives Ray her first full status report, one month into the project. She has selected the core technologies, identified key advocates within the organization and started to identify areas where the company can save both time and money. In particular, she highlights ways for teams to cut costs:

- Eliminate contractors through more effective use of existing employees.
- If you are able improve efficiency enough to do the work without certain hires, leave salaries for those positions open. Recruiting costs for those positions will then be zero.
- Use attrition to reduce headcount for a few current positions that will not be filled because of efficiencies that can be gained through these techniques.
- Reduce temporary and permanent relocation costs and travel costs between locations.
- Reduce recruiting costs and lost productivity that might have otherwise been incurred due to an employee leaving because of lifestyle reasons.

CHAPTER 10:
THE NEW BUSINESS PROCESSES

Sandra now turns to the processes she thinks need to change to improve efficiency, as well as how the team can measure those improvements. She's had a couple of Internet meetings with Li and one of Li's managers to talk about their processes in more detail and to review Sandra's ideas for how to change the business. Chris is working with Sandra and her team nearly full-time, but Li is a tremendous sounding board and continues to be very generous with her time.

Through these meetings, the advocates Sandra is working with got some first-hand experience with the tools, and they really started to see the possibilities quickly, Sandra reports. They even stored project plans and brainstorming notes on the project collaboration database with the help of one of Chris' consultants.

As Sandra and Chris have looked at the business practices, they've continuously updated the benefits and the values. Based on input from Chris and Li, Sandra believes that they need to formalize some of their common processes and create a few new ones. These are the processes she thinks are most affected:

- Project portfolio
- Project planning
- Communicating the plan
- Resource and skills inventory
- Project staffing
- Project startup
- Assignment and supervision of work
- Team walk-throughs
- Brainstorming and design sessions
- Status meetings
- Problem identification and problem resolution
- Escalation
- Running multiple project initiatives

"This is a lot of detail, but I think we need to talk briefly about each of the processes and how they are different in a distributed environment," Sandra concludes. "We expect to get some resistance, and it will be important for you to support the team when the holdouts start to ask why they can't do things the way they've always done them."

Project Portfolio. The team found that about 75 percent of the work is fairly well accounted for. People are getting projects approved, and they do a reasonably good job of staying within budget. However, there are still a fair number of skunk works projects and times when a project consumes more resources than planned. One of the keys to making the best use of resources is for management to know that people are working on the right projects and to put in place an early warning system to detect when projects are running over. This is also key to staffing across projects.

Project Planning. Major projects are reasonably well-planned, but a lot of time is lost on small projects and on early startup before people have put controls in place. The team sees tremendous value in teaching best practices on planning for small and large projects and having those projects stored on the project collaboration environment and reviewed frequently. That's not dramatically different from the way things are done now, but it is important to bring all of the work under governance, so that management can get a view of the total portfolio.

Communicating the Plan. Some of the biggest changes will be around the issues of communication and supervision. While the company does a good job of communicating project objectives and plans among the leadership, it needs to do a better job of communicating the project objectives, scope and deliverables to all of the project team members. This is crucial, because remote team members can't drift by the project manager's desk and see the project plan hanging on the wall or strike up a casual conversation to clarify a point of confusion. As Chris and Li's experience has shown, the casual conversations will come as people get used to sending an instant message and picking up the phone for a quick call.

Also, remote teams are often operating in different time zones. Every team member must be able to see the scope of the project, how it will be successful, the plan and deliverables and how his or her work will contribute to making the project successful. That way, no matter where they are and what time zone they are in, team members have a clear framework to understand the project and their role. The new process sets this up to communicate the plan in several ways:

- First, the team will be much more formal in documenting the project charter and project plan independent of the size of the project. That information gets stored in the project collaboration environment, where team members can regularly review the definition of success of the project.
- Second, any time the scope and measurable objectives of the project are changed, the project leader needs to modify them under version control. That way, the entire team shifts with the change and there are no misunderstandings among the sponsors, the project managers and the team members, no matter where the team is located.
- Third, the team needs to use the meeting manager to walk through the project charter and plan with everyone involved,

allowing people to ask questions, understand the purpose of the project and the plan and identify areas where they can make suggestions or ask for clarifications. Clarifications and changes need to be reviewed with the team and stored on the project collaboration environment as an updated version of the charter and plan.

- Finally, things change, people forget or their memory of the agreements shifts over time. Therefore, about every two weeks the team should revisit the current scope of the project and the project plan and agree that either nothing has changed, or that the project charter and plan need to be updated to keep the written agreements consistent with what is actually being done.

"We believe this is a much richer communication strategy than we have in place on most projects. It will benefit all of our teams, but it will be critical to those that are run at a distance," Sandra says. "We believe that a better understanding of the work is one of the major sources of efficiency. From our early analysis, we find that over time we can eliminate 5 to 10 percent of the labor in some of our largest projects through rework that will not occur if people have a better understanding of what they are doing and why, and if they have better control over the overall objectives of the project."

Ray responds, "Well, I can certainly see the benefits. But frankly, Sandra, that seems a little complex. Many of our engineers will feel that it stifles their creativity and adds a level of bureaucracy to their work. Are you sure you will be able to get people to adopt this process?"

"Actually," Sandra replies, "when we ran this by our team members, several of them showed us documents that looked just like our project charters. Communication and understanding doesn't stifle creativity; they channel it. When a person has a great new idea, we want him or her to talk to the team and the sponsor about it. If it doesn't fit, let's kill it early so we don't waste time. If it's a great idea, then let's fund it appropriately so it gets done right."

"I certainly support those principles," Ray says. "But I can see that this will be one of the points where we need to improve understanding in order to get change. Let's go on, and we'll watch this as it unfolds."

Resource and Skills Inventory. Along with project staffing, this is another area that will change substantially. The division tends to be very hierarchical and team-organized right now. It is broken up into product groups, and the groups have individual staff and projects. Projects rarely span two groups and almost never span two locations. A large initiative or program might be made up of multiple projects, but even then is kept within a specific campus. When a team is missing a resource, it doesn't think to look outside of its own campus or even outside its own group for help.

Having some people underutilized in one team or location while using staff who are mismatched to a role or using expensive contractors to get work done at another leads to one of the greatest losses in effectiveness. One of the key enabling technologies in the project collaboration environment is a skills inventory that allows a manager to look first in his or her own group, then across groups for the best talent fit. Since a manager can assign and supervise staff at a distance, it will be important to assess where the best talent lies and to do far more resource-sharing between locations and groups.

One of the skills that needs to be quantified is the ability to manage or work on remote projects. While that will necessarily become a core competence for most managers and many employees over a year or two, working and managing remotely is not a skill that is uniformly available today. Until it becomes a standard skill, the company will also need to offer training and mentoring in this area.

Staffing Projects. The process of selecting staff for a project begins by having a plan that identifies the work and an estimate of the labor and skills necessary to do the work. Some work requires very specific skills and, in some cases, specific individuals who can lead or perform the work. Other work is more general. For example, with some of the leading-edge products, there are a handful of engineers and software specialists who are critical to advancing the product. Once those people are properly assigned, the balance of the project can be staffed with more general resources.

Chris and Li have been very helpful in discussing how to get people to accept the concept of remote workers and remote teams. At Li's company, they staff projects completely independent of geography and look exclusively at skills. Employees are so used to collaborating over the Internet that being together is just not an issue. Also, they have additional technologies like electronic whiteboards and Web cams almost everywhere, so it is really just like being in the same office. While having teams work that distributed in the first six to 12 months is probably not realistic, it will become more comfortable for most people after a year or so.

In the interim, Chris suggests they start with small teams, with a team leader physically co-located reporting to the overall project manager. Once people are comfortable with that level of distribution, the company can expand gradually until geography is irrelevant. Chris believes that if they make geography a non-issue in assignments over time, that in 12 to 18 months, the company will be able to assign almost any staff person to any team and get the project to work. They may also use single workers who are totally remote from the rest of a team if that person is a specialist or if they have a role that lends itself well to working remotely, such as market research, documentation and training development or quality testing in areas like software.

This is an area where the company will mature over time, so it is essential to establish metrics to assure that productivity is increasing.

Based on Chris' analysis, fully 2 percent of the 5 to 6 percent target savings will come from using the right person regardless of geography.

Project Startup. Thinking back to Chris' earlier diagram of what work should be done remotely and what should be done in person, project startup is one of those areas that is best done in person whenever possible.

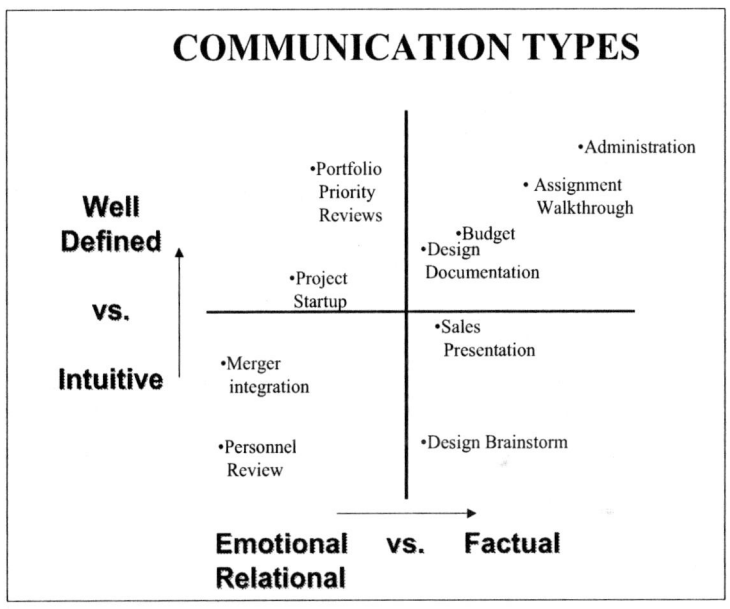

First, most of the work during project startup is very intuitive. The leaders are still trying to figure out what is the ultimate objective of the project, how they will know they are successful and the best approach to the work. Second, team members may be coming together for the first time, and they need to learn about each other, their respective strengths and weaknesses and their respective personalities. All of these tasks fall into the intuitive and emotional/relational quadrant.

There are a few notable exceptions. If the project planning exercise is the next phase of a major program in which most of the team remains the same, then that can be done apart because the work is understood and the team is already working together. Also, if it takes more than a few days to build a very detailed plan, then that is moving toward the part of the work that is well-understood and very factual. In that case, the project or program leadership team can come together for a few days to get to know each other and then again to agree on the final plan. The detailed planning can certainly be done remotely.

Finally, when you staff up and add the bulk of the project team members, that's also an important time to bring the team together in one place. The team members can get to know one another well and develop an understanding of the scope of the project, the plan and their role within the plan. After that, most communication can be run remotely. However, if the project runs for more than a few months, it is useful to get together periodically to develop trust, reinforce personal relationships and work out personality issues. Although Sandra expects a small increase in travel, it is more than offset by making better use of people and decreasing the use of contractors.

Assignment and Supervision of Work. Of course, it is essential that each person understands the deliverable that he or she needs to produce, where to get source information for the work and where to store the output of the work. Assignment reviews and supervisory walk-throughs at the beginning of the work, at the completion and occasionally throughout the performance in order to resolve issues are also important. The Internet meeting manager is a perfect tool for these walk-throughs.

It's also important to replace the physical workplace so that someone who is struggling can get help immediately. At Li's company, when people have an idea that they want to discuss or a problem they need help with, they can just send an instant message to the person they need to talk to. A brief description of the problem is enough to start a conversation or set up a time to talk later. Then, they can launch an Internet meeting and begin working on the problem within minutes. If they are brainstorming, they can just go to a whiteboard room. After a while, people seem to accept this approach. The implementation team has only had these tools for a few weeks, and people are already feeling comfortable.

Team Walk-throughs. Frequently, the entire team needs to do reviews of part of the work. The same tools used for day-to-day supervision work for these reviews, too. The team leader schedules a walk-through in the calendar and gets everyone on a conference call and an Internet meeting. Never again will the team need to wait until everyone can get to the same city to do a walk-through or a review. This, plus brainstorming on the Internet, can take a month out of the development cycles, saving precious time and money.

Brainstorming and Design Sessions. Brainstorming is not one of those things that are easily done from a distance. It is a very intuitive process, and it requires people to maintain their focus for a long time. However, this is really where electronic whiteboards become important. An electronic whiteboard is just like a regular whiteboard. If two or more of them are connected through an Internet meeting, participants can actually pass control back and forth. It has a slide sorter, just like PowerPoint, so you don't have to erase the board to make another point; you just open another slide. You can go forward, backward or jump around to make a point.

Sandra doesn't want to force this technology too early, but she plans to create electronic whiteboard conference rooms and even put a few in the home of a remote worker or two. Li's team took a year or more to get comfortable with the whiteboards, but people eventually got there, and Sandra is confident her team will as well. The real value is not just saving travel costs, but saving time.

Status Reports and Status Meetings. A status report is just a deliverable, and a status meeting is just a walk-through. So the same tools and techniques discussed in team walk-throughs are applicable to status reports and status meetings. The team prepares the deliverable, conducts the walk-through meeting and stores the updated deliverable on the project collaboration system.

Problem Identification and Problem Solving. This area and escalation, which is next, run together. The project collaboration environment really helps with problem identification within the issue and risk management capabilities. By recording an issue or a risk, any project member is able to surface a problem, escalate that problem to another team member or management and then record the alternatives and the ultimate resolution. The project team can track the issues and problems that are open so that they do not slip through the cracks. But real problem solving doesn't occur in email or even in the project collaboration environment. Problem solving occurs when two or more smart people begin to interact and collaborate on the problem resolution. Most of that work occurs interactively. Sandra has developed eight basic steps for resolving problems:

1. Record the problem in the issues management system in the project collaboration environment and assign that problem to the team members or management members who can most effectively resolve the problem.
2. Prepare documentation around the problem and attach it to the issue in the project collaboration environment so that everything is in one place.
3. Schedule a problem-solving session with all of the appropriate parties.
4. Run the problem-solving meeting using the Internet meeting manager so that all participants are looking at exactly the same material from wherever they are.

5. Begin the meeting with a clear definition of success. For example, "This discussion will be successful if all team members understand the problem, we are able to assign research assignments and we schedule the final problem resolution meeting." Everyone knows exactly is expected and can check off each step.
6. Conduct the meeting as a walk-through, changing the materials on meeting manager so that everyone has seen and agreed to the same written materials.
7. Store the results of the meeting on the project collaboration environment as either progress or a final resolution of the issue.
8. Schedule the work and the next meeting necessary to complete the resolution of the problem. Repeat this process until everyone is comfortable that the problem is solved.

While this seems like a lot of steps, they are really simple and constantly drive the problem toward resolution, especially in light of the current process. Currently, the person who identifies the problem sends an email to let people know that a problem exists. Other well-intentioned people reply to the email, involving an ever-increasing number of people. Often, a protracted email debate occurs as people simply agree to disagree in successive emails. Equally often, the problem slips through the cracks as people get busy and assume that someone else is handling it. This new process assures that the problem is assigned and tracked, that people come together and reach resolution and that the resolution is recorded in writing so that everyone remembers the resolution the same way. The bottom line is that problems get solved faster, with more certainty and far less emotion.

Escalation. Last, a formal process for escalation is important. The purpose of any escalation technique is to assure that problems don't fester and damage the project or the working relationships of the people. First, a problem is recorded and the team attempts to work through the normal problem-solving process. When a problem is not solved quickly, it may need to be escalated through management until it reaches the level where it can be solved. That can be done in the project collaboration environment simply by adding the name of the leader to whom it is escalated on the issue assignment list and designating that person as the escalation party. Serious issues can be escalated until they reach the person who can bring them to closure. No one loses track of the issue, to whom it's assigned or the alternatives that have been considered.

"Well, Sandra, this has been a little overwhelming, but I understand it," says Ray. "It follows the logic that we have used for well-organized processes throughout the division, except that it adds geographies and time zones. I can't see where you will get any pushback from our leadership team. This is a nice piece of work."

Chapter 10 Takeaways

Sandra assesses the company's existing business practices and identifies 12 that will need to change in order for it to succeed as a distributed company. They can be divided into four general categories that are applicable across many different types of companies:

1. Doing the right work with good plans and good teams
   - Project portfolio
   - Project planning
   - Communicating the plan
2. Allocating the work to the right team members, then assigning and supervising the work across geographies and time zones
   - Resource and skills inventory
   - Project staffing
3. Effective communication within the team, whether that is a few team members working together on a single deliverable, or the entire team doing a status update
   - Project startup
   - Assignment and supervision of work
   - Team walk-throughs
   - Brainstorming and design sessions
   - Status meetings
4. Effective problem identification, problem solving and escalation that will keep a project moving smoothly across geographies and time zones

The New Business Processes

- Problem identification and problem resolution
- Escalation

Chapter 11: Picking Projects

"OK," Sandra says. "Before we talk about our pilot projects, we need to understand that the processes we've discussed are equally important whether they apply to a single project or a multiple-project initiative."

When there are multiple projects within an initiative, the processes must apply to all of the same disciplines, Sandra explains. But often, leaders do not report to the same boss or organization. This makes it hard to get consensus and closure on objectives and plans and to resolve issues.

To illustrate her point, Sandra mentions a current initiative by Alpha Corp. to ship a major new product. Several of the projects within the initiative involve changing the components that make up the product.

Also within the initiative are one or more software projects. Finally, there are sub-contractors, suppliers and other internal departments such as marketing and manufacturing that are all working on the project.

"Empowering the program manager to direct all of those people is frequently difficult," she says. Therefore—in order to be sure that their processes scale to that size—the team needs to make sure that some portion of the pilot projects comes from within a complex initiative.

After that cautionary note, Sandra moves on to the final topic for the day: picking projects. "We want to pick about 10 pilot projects that give us a good cross-section of work from the division," she says. She hands Ray a list of programs and projects that includes 10 highlighted items.

She explains that in designing a cross-section, her team has tried to get the following mix:

- A few complex projects run by excellent project managers to ensure that the new processes are efficient and add value to the best and brightest employees ("This will also help us to make them advocates," she notes.)
- A few simple projects to prove that the techniques scale down to all of the division's projects (the idea being to prevent people from trying to get their projects declared as too small to be measured and managed this way)

- A mix of projects that are just getting started and projects that are already underway, in order to make sure that the techniques can be applied to all projects, not just large, new ones
- A mix of projects that are stand-alone and projects that are part of a larger initiative, to prove that the processes can work on major efforts
- A few projects that are under the leadership of people who are likely to be stubborn about keeping things the way they have always been. ("Let's let them participate and get their objections on the table early so that we can address them right away," Sandra says.)

Ray scans the list, suggests a few small changes and signs off on the choices.

"Well, Ray, we said this meeting would be a success if we did the following," Sandra says:

- Review the project plan and the current status against the 12-step process that Chris outlined for us at our last meeting.
- Get your approval of the list of advocates that we have selected to lead the change in the division.
- Get your feedback and approval on the business values that we have targeted to achieve during the first phase of the implementation.

- Listen to your feedback on the business practices that the team feels must change.
- Get your approval on the target projects that we will use to validate our business practice changes.

"Have we accomplished the objectives of today's meeting, and are we ready to go forward with the design and implementation phase of the program?" Sandra asks.

"I think this is excellent," Ray responds. "Chris, you've been noticeably silent in today's meeting. What do you think?" he asks.

"I simply didn't have anything to add," Chris explains. "Sandra and her core team have been very talented clients. As you can see, the processes that Sandra has recommended are very much your standard processes, but with some added formality and adaptation based upon the best practices that we have brought to the table. I think it is far more effective when the changes are led and presented by your leaders, rather than by me."

Chris concludes by assuring Ray that he and his colleagues have worked closely with Sandra to this point and are confident that these processes will work in Ray's shop. "But thanks for asking," he says.

"OK," says Ray. "If there are no further points for today, then let's proceed with the project as planned meet again formally in three to four weeks."

Chapter 11 Takeaways

Sandra notes that the processes she and her team have identified are equally important whether they apply to a single project or a multiple-project initiative. In order to make sure that the new processes are effective for a variety of initiatives—including complex, multi-discipline ones—**it's important to pilot a range of projects:**

1. Complex projects run by excellent managers to ensure that the new processes add value to the best and brightest
2. Projects that are just getting started and projects that are already underway, to ensure the techniques can be applied to all projects, not just large, new ones
3. Projects that are stand-alone and projects that are part of a larger initiative, to prove that the processes can work on major efforts
4. Projects led by people who are likely to be stubborn about keeping things the way they have always been

CHAPTER 12:
EARLY IMPLEMENTATION: LESSONS ABOUT PEOPLE & PROCESSES

We rejoin our team a couple of months into its live operations, at which point there are 10 projects up and running. Before applying the new principles to all of product development and suggesting to Marvin that they be used on an even broader basis, the team feels it's important to examine lessons learned thus far.

Sandra begins the meeting. "Ray, this meeting will be successful if we can update you on our progress to date, talk about some lessons learned and how they will impact our future progress, identify some critical areas where we need your help and get your agreement that it is time to go to Marvin with a status report and a plan for the rest of the company."

"Wow, another very full set of objectives," responds Ray. "Are you going to let Chris talk some this time?"

"Actually, yes," says Sandra, and explains that some of the lessons the team has learned so far are ones that Chris had anticipated from working with previous customers. "So he set us up to build on the lessons that they had learned," she explains, "although some of the lessons we ended up with are new even to him."

Sandra pulls out the now familiar 12-step process and reminds everyone that since the first six major steps had already been completed, the goal of the pilot projects was to work on steps seven through 12. She then quickly reminds them of the remaining steps:

> 7. Train people on the technologies and the business practices at the same time.
> 8. Execute our pilot programs and projects with the new procedures.
> 9. Measure our results and adjust the processes.
> 10. Expand the number of people and programs involved.
> 11. Expand to new processes that add incremental value.
> 12. Learn the limits of when we get diminishing returns and stop there until our people are ready to stretch the boundaries again.

Ray interrupts, "Before we get too far into this, how are the pilot projects going? Are we getting the business results we were aiming for?"

"Fair question," Sandra responds. "We think the answer to that is a cautious 'yes.' But we really need to stay on top of the pilots for the next six months or so to make sure that the changes stick and that we harvest the benefits." Sandra then gives a rundown of what's happening with the 10 pilot projects:

- Three projects are going well and are fully up to speed. They are already experiencing a reduction in contractor head count and improvements in time to project completion. By the end of six months, they will be at or beyond our target objectives.
- Four projects are going OK. They seem to have surmounted the learning curve and are starting to show thorough adoption of the new processes. They should begin to yield results in another month or two, which means they should be close to our target objectives at the end of six months.
- Two projects are struggling a bit. They resisted the changes at first, complaining that the virtual environment was a distraction, and asked to go back to their old processes. Now they are accepting the changes, but slowly. As the other projects succeed, they are seeing that this can work. We think they will be slightly behind our target goals at the end of six months but will have reached them by the nine-month mark.
- One project is failing. The manager is a complete holdout. His remote teams feel they are ignored and given the least important work. This project is behind schedule, over budget and unlikely

to succeed unless we make some leadership changes or let the team go back to working physically in the same place.

"Ray," Chris adds, "these are about the results that we see in most companies." He explains that some of Ray's managers are very aligned with the business objectives; they jump in and embrace the change and take to the changes like birds take to flight. Others will learn and are progressing at varying rates. "Some will resist until they figure out that these changes won't go away," he says, "and occasionally you get someone who simply can't or won't adjust."

Sandra explains that the training has been completed and that the pilot programs are well underway. Therefore, the lessons learned so far come from both the training and the pilot programs, as well as from talking to advocates who are preparing their groups to go next.

"The training went well," Sandra says. "The technology was easy to learn, we had very active participants and we got great feedback on the business processes. Sometimes lessons learned are positive reinforcement of the things that you did right. Chris gave us some solid coaching, and we think there were several key factors in the success of the training."

According to Sandra, there are four critical success factors. They actually must happen in the following order, and each level of achievement brings another level of success:

- Line managers buying-in, encouraging and supporting
- Line managers embracing and energizing both their local teams and their remote team members equally
- Doing the right things to train, build and support the team
- Getting the individual team members collaborating remotely peer-to-peer, without communicating only through the management chain

Line managers buy-in, encouragement and support. First and foremost, people must believe that these changes are important to the company and to their own careers and personal goals, Chris says. "There are a few of the managers who just don't think this is a good idea, and they've decided not to spend the time to make it work. In one case, the manager is stonewalling the change, hoping it will go away," he says.

"Is that the case in the project that's failing?" Ray asks.

"It's the primary reason," Sandra answers. She then outlines the project manager's history for Ray. Because of the need to help develop a particular software component, she and Chris tried to leverage some of the company's offshore development team in India working with a team in the California office. But Dave, the manager of the project, believes strongly that people are best managed within 50 feet of his desk. He objected strongly to the changes from the beginning and said he felt sure he would have trouble making deadlines. Chris and Sandra discussed the situation with his superior right away, and decided that working closely with this manager would be critical. "As we've monitored the situation, we've found some patterns," Sandra says.

First of all, Dave tends to think poorly of people from other teams and other locations. In fact, there have been multiple conversations during which he or a member of his inner circle has criticized someone from another team as incompetent. Later, however, when some of those same people physically joined his team, he became their biggest supporter. Why? The employees moved to within 50 feet of his desk, and they began reporting directly to him in the organization chart. When asked about this pattern, the manager said, "We like to build cults of productivity, and to do that, we have to be together." Furthermore, he has not traveled a single time during the project.

Second, his supervision style is extremely informal. He relies largely on verbal explanations and communicates specifications sketchily. He makes changes without documenting them and has a history of surprising product management with undocumented changes to products that are caught only during quality assurance or at the customer site.

Finally, Dave tends to review work by taking it back to his desk and examining it, frequently changing it and giving it back to employees the way he wanted it without explaining the changes. He is not a particularly good teacher or developer of people.

EARLY IMPLEMENTATION

"So why have we kept someone with these kinds of work habits for as long as we have?" asks Ray. "It sounds like his problems run much deeper than not being able to run remote teams."

Sandra agrees but notes that Dave is valued by many of the company's leaders for his ability to get very innovative work done quickly.

"You know, Ray, this is not uncommon," Chris interjects. "We frequently find that introducing new concepts, such as distributed teams or Six Sigma Quality exposes core problems that have existed for a long time in the organization." According to Chris, when the processes start to fail, they're often blamed until someone like Sandra goes back and looks at the root cause of the problem. "Then you find the leaders that have resisted anything that looks like a formal process and have expected the rest of the organization to adapt to them. Sometimes these leaders are gifted enough to make exceptions for. In other cases, either their behavior must change, or they need to be replaced."

"OK, I see," responds Ray. "So what's your recommendation?"

Sandra explains that this is an issue they want to delegate to Ray. She and Chris have prepared an analysis of the situation and are hoping Ray will talk to the project manager and his boss. If the manager doesn't change his behavior, they would like to move him back into a design-engineering role and replace him as the leader of the project. "Otherwise, we'll be rewarding someone for stonewalling the change, and we think that could be a negative example for other people that don't want to change," Sandra says.

"All right," agrees Ray. "Give me the briefing book. I'll speak with his manager first, and then with him."

"Thanks, Ray," says Sandra. "Sorry to give you the tough ones. But this will show that you are unconditionally behind the changes, and that will help a lot."

Line managers embrace and energize both their local and remote team members equally. According to Chris, there are some fundamental truths about running distributed teams that involve style and belief more than process and technology. "Let's talk about some of those and how they are affecting the projects that are struggling or failing," he says, and outlines a list:

- Communication on any project must be frequent, and it must be both formal and informal.
- Although the staff can stay home, the leaders of virtual projects must travel.
- Managers must use regular walk-throughs to assign work, review the completion of work and monitor the progress of tasks.
- People must believe that these changes are important to the company and to their own careers and personal goals.

Chris then explains each of these truths in turn, starting with the importance of **frequent communication on any project,** both formal and informal. "The tools certainly exist for that," he says. Formal communications can occur with Internet meetings that are scheduled on everyone's calendar. Informal communication can be initiated with a phone call or an instant message that simply says, "Got a minute?"

Some of the managers of the struggling projects are less communicative than their peers, Chris says. He and Sandra are working with those managers to get them comfortable with the idea that they must initiate formal communication and be accessible for informal communication on a regular basis. The pilot projects that are succeeding are those with the most communicative and accessible managers. In contrast, those that are struggling tend to be led by people who are very uncomfortable with formal communication and poor at informal communication. The poor communicators send a lot of emails and when the team introduced them to instant messenger, they began to use it like email to send messages in writing.

"Right now, we are giving those managers additional training and coaching to teach them how to talk with their people to motivate and to clarify and then how and when to convert the informal discussions to written deliverables," Chris says.

Second, because managing by walking around is one of the things that suffers in the virtual environment, **the leaders of virtual projects must**

travel. Travel doesn't have to be burdensome or extensive, but leaders need to visit employees at their home location rather than fly them into headquarters. "That way, employees sense that geography is not an issue in their careers." Chris says. Among the pilot projects that are doing best, more than half of the leaders come from backgrounds where travel was the norm (e.g. consulting, sales and product management), he explains. Among the projects that are struggling, more than half of the leaders think of travel as burdensome and an exception to the rule. "The correlation is not 100 percent, as it is with communication skills, but it's very high," Chris says.

Third, **managers must use regular walk-throughs** to assign work, review the completion of work and monitor the progress of tasks, Chris says. Supervision of remote workers requires a fairly formal and interactive process, he explains. When he and Sandra outlined the process for assignment and supervision of work, they talked about the importance of these regular walk-throughs. Leaders who were used to formal supervision and who knew how much supervision an individual employee requires took to the process immediately. Those who were less formal are having some difficulty getting their employees to understand what is expected of them, he says.

Sandra goes on to explain that they had found an excellent example of a struggling team that got over it and they were using it as an example for the other teams that were struggling. Betty was the leader of a team. She was in the London center and had team members in both Detroit and

India. She struggled establishing informal communication with her remote teams and the team leaders there found that they were given less important roles and they felt left out of the camaraderie that they saw with the team in London.

Whenever there was a problem, Betty called a meeting in London, placing the burden on the remote teams to travel to her. The people from the London team were fresh and well-prepared, while the remote team members were tired from travel. Also, the remote team members observed first hand the camaraderie of the people that worked in one location.

Carol, the team leader from Detroit, pointed this out to Chris in one of the team debriefings. When we talked to Betty about it, she was completely unaware. We taught her to reach out more frequently in informal chats with her remote leaders, to make sure that she was balancing the challenging assignments and to spend one week every month with either her team in India or her team in Detroit. Also we taught her to solve problems with the Internet meeting tools to have people flying in for fewer crisis meetings.

The results: The travel budget for the team went down. The remote teams immediately felt more bonded with Betty and her other leaders and this is now one of the projects that is coming up to speed and gaining productivity weekly.

Doing the right things to train, build and support the team. The next greatest critical success factor is training and coaching the team members. All of the highest performing teams in the pilot have gotten this and the management issues right.

The first key is to **start each training session with the business reasons** behind the new processes and tools. This makes it fairly easy to talk about the new practices and to adopt them quickly. It's tempting to think that team members need only to know the processes and tools, or even just the tools, Sandra explains. "But Chris made sure that if we had to shorten the training, *we never eliminated the business case conversation*," she says.

Once people understand why the changes are being made and how the success of the new practices would be measured, the staff started contributing their own suggestions almost daily! Most of those suggestions were very positive, and almost all of the staff are now focused on ways to make the business measurably more effective. "Teaching the tools and technology was always the last step and, in some cases, almost an afterthought," Sandra says. "We believe that focusing on the 'why' question is critical in future training."

We've also discovered that **using senior managers to lead the business case discussions** and conversations about business practices conveyed an important message to the staff: If these processes were important enough for managers to invest their time in—and use themselves—then the practices were going to become a serious part of the way people worked in the future.

We taught the managers first, and then engaged the staff with their managers in the training room. To be efficient with the managers' time, we had them attend to business case discussions and conversations about business practices; then, when we looked at the technology, we let them leave.

Sandra pauses for a moment to reflect on the past. "Remember when you and I were project team members? We'd get these mystery directives from management, but with little information to back them. How often did those ever change anything?"

Ray pauses to think for a moment, "Hardly ever. I can see your point."

Doing a large percentage of the early training in person was important for gaining trust and changing behavior. We started out thinking that we would do a lot of Web training since the tools are Web tools and we want to get people thinking about the power of the Web. Chris made us realize that the initial training is about trust and behavior, and that these goals are very deep in the intuitive work and relationship-building quadrant. We looked hard at the outcome we wanted in terms of belief, and change in behavior and decided to do much of the early training in person. We found that worked well, and we recommend continuing with that approach.

We tried to train one of our most technically proficient teams remotely. They picked up the technology, but then dropped it just as quick. In different session that we did live, we had a mixed crowd, including a few people who could barely do more than check their email and type a word document. One of the guys even had his arms crossed tight over his chest and a glare in his eyes that clearly said, "There isn't a thing you can teach me." Two days later, we were in a training meeting, all in the same room, but using the meeting center for the hands on and comfort experience. In the middle of the session, he yelled out, "Wow!" and started bringing up different systems that the group is responsible for monitoring and maintaining, pointing at things with the mouse and in general showing *everyone else* how much easier their jobs would be. The second group hasn't shown any signs of slowing. Since then, we've gone back to the other group and conducted a live training session, and we had the same response.

Later on we noticed that **including many of our standard business methods in the training** created added benefit. "When we started," she says, "we thought we had pretty strong methodologies. What we found is that we have highly variable implementation and use of those methods." As it turns out, Sandra explains, small projects use their own processes. Many managers brought their own methods with them when they joined the company, and only vaguely follow Alpha Corp.'s standard processes. "Therefore, we spent a fair amount of time bringing people up to speed on our standard methods so that we could tell when the problems that surfaced were based on team members being remote, and when they were based on bad process or poor supervision," Sandra says. "We think the methods are in pretty good shape now, but we need to bring those methods and the 'being there' processes and tools under the same leadership."

Chris adds that having well-understood and well-followed methods and processes will become even more important as the changes are introduced to other parts of the company. In his work with previous clients, he's found that divisions such as manufacturing, marketing and sales frequently have good approaches for everyday work, but are far more ad hoc around project initiatives such as launching a new product or a new sales campaign. "As Sandra learned, if you don't have good processes that are well-understood and followed reasonably well, then the distributed work environment becomes a good whipping boy for failures that would have happened anyway," he says.

According to Chris, if Ray's division wants to be the focal point of change in the company (in terms of building and executing virtual teams), it must get its own processes in order and help peers in other divisions to do the same. "That will allow you to measure results rather than effort and attendance—something that's key in the distributed world."

"I think I understand," responds Ray, "but frankly, I'm surprised to find that we aren't following our own methodologies. It certainly seems that we are every time that I review a project."

"I hear you," says Sandra. "Chris and I had some fairly heated discussions about this topic early on." Like Ray, Sandra had felt confident that the division's teams were following standard company methods. But she soon discovered that although many employees were good at producing plans and status reports that followed the basic methods, actual use of the methods below the most basic levels was spotty—partly because employee training was inadequate.

"As we add distance and organizational boundaries, it's critical that people understand the work they are doing, the deliverables they are producing and how it all fits together," she adds. "We've found that adding a half day of training on the company's basic methods helped with this a lot. This leads nicely into some of the other major success factors."

Giving people the opportunity to use the new processes and technology immediately after being taught meant that they quickly became part of the fiber of the way people work. We had project managers set up practice scenarios using the meeting center, and we got each of the projects onto the project collaboration environment as soon as they finished the training. That way, there was no leakage in knowledge or belief as people went back to their old ways of doing things. In cases where we weren't ready to use the new processes right away, we found that we had to go back and do brush-up training before moving to the new practices. Even then, the projects were slightly slower to pick up the processes and tools.

Finally, assigning mentors to each project team helped the teams to adopt the use of the new technology and processes after training was complete. Because mentoring is usually a part-time assignment, we found that a mentor can support three to four mid-size project teams or one to two large teams at a time. In addition, because we have built the belief within the teams that planning and execution can be taught and reinforced one-on-one and in small groups using the meeting center, mentors can work remotely.

"All in all," finishes Sandra, "we think that we got broad acceptance from handling it this way, and we want to be sure to keep following these steps as we roll out the processes through the rest of the groups." She adds that because there is always a desire to shortcut training and change management, one of the goals of today's meeting is to get Ray's agreement to the rollout budget that they sent him. Once he does that, her team will be able to put trainers on-site with the next wave of project teams, which will follow the initial pilots.

"We found this one out by accident. We had about half a dozen local teams go live within a month of each other. Relatively speaking, they all looked to have the same success potential. They all did at least OK, but whenever the one specific team was involved, all of the teams became more productive. It turns out the project that was creating the strongest impact had a young process engineer on the project that kept coming up with ways to help people make their jobs easier. Since he kept being right, the rest of the team kept listening."

We pulled him off the project, much to the chagrin of the project manager, and set him to mentor all of the teams on the project. Sure enough, all of the teams came up to the same speed. This was the first project to really hit stride."

Ray asks how that strategy impacts the overall project cost and return on investment.

According to Sandra, it's within the initial project budget. She adds that because the new processes are gaining fast acceptance, the time to return on investment will be further accelerated. "It's a very cost-effective process," she says.

Getting the individual team members collaborating remotely peer-to-peer, without working up through the management chain. While the leading projects have not fully reached this point, several pockets have started to form. By working directly with one another, they recover much of the wasted time lost waiting for management approval and the extra steps in the communications process.

We've even had an outstanding example where this really paid off: Not a week before the training announcement went out, Steve, one of our top sales engineers, put in his notice that he was leaving. You see, Steve is so good that he keeps getting sent on location for the critical projects. But, Steve also has two kids, whom he hardly ever sees during the week. His manager couldn't find a way to make it work, so Steve put in his notice.

When his manager found out, he called Steve at home and told him that he had been assigned to a pilot project using technology that would enable him to travel less than 35 percent of the time. Steve agreed to stay on until training was over, just to see. It worked even better than we hoped. Steve now works remotely with three younger sales engineers who all show promise. So, instead of losing a top guy, he's the remote expert and mentor for three younger staffers, who are all growing faster as a result, and supporting 10 times as many sales engagements.

"Sounds like you guys have made some great progress," says Ray.

"Thank you," says Sandra. She also asks Ray to review some of the best projects as well as some of those that are struggling. She thinks that if people see that Ray is watching them closely, they will adapt and bring their performance to a higher level.

"Consider it done," says Ray.

"Great," says Chris, adding that he has recorded the issues they've discussed in the project collaboration environment. They're now on Ray's home page, and as he addresses each one, he can update the status so Chris and Sandra will know when he is done.

"The only things left," adds Sandra, "are to get approval to roll out the changes to the rest of product development and to consider going to Marvin with a status report.

CHAPTER 12 TAKEAWAYS

Sandra and Chris identified the following as **key success factors** in benefiting the most from the new processes and technologies:

1. Line managers buying-in, encouraging and supporting the changes
    a. People must believe that these changes are important.
2. Line managers embracing and energizing both their local teams and their remote team members equally
    a. Frequent communication on any project
    b. Management "by walking around"
    c. Regular walkthroughs
3. Doing the right things to train, build and support the team
    a. Start each training session with the business reasons.
    b. Use senior managers to lead the business case discussions.
    c. Do a large percentage of the early training in person.
    d. Include many standard business methodologies in the training.
    e. Give people the opportunity to use the processes and technologies immediately.
    f. Assign mentors to each project team.
4. Getting the individual team members collaborating remotely peer-to-peer, without working up through the management chain

a. Let top performers become mentors to remote juniors.

Chapter 13:

Managing Across Department & Corporate Boundaries

A few months later, Ray, Sandra and her team sit with Chris in Marvin's office. After coming to the last slide in her presentation, Sandra asks Ray to summarize the status of the pilot projects.

"Marvin, we've progressed further than I could have thought possible," Ray begins. "Our initial pilot projects are all beginning to show measurable economic success, and we are well on our way to achieving several of the objectives that outlined when we started this program."

Ray explains that the pilot projects initially lost some productivity due to startup costs, but once people learned how to use the new technologies and business practices, things improved. "Now that the teams are up to speed, we are seeing tangible benefits," he says, and notes the following:

- There are now multiple projects running in multiple locations, with teams achieving the same productivity as if they were traveling. Through savings on travel, relocation and the use of contractors (no longer necessary because employees from remote locations can be used), the pilots have almost completely covered the cost of the project.
- The company's offshore development center is being used effectively, and is achieving almost 90 percent of the productivity that occurs when teams are in a single location. Furthermore, because the company no longer relocates contractors from India to work on-site, the division is able to use those employees in India and save almost $60,000 per employee per year. A side benefit is that the company no longer has to worry about the immigration process for employees traveling on site from India. As a result, months' time has been saved on two critical projects, improving both cost and time to market.
- Management processes, already strong, are becoming more finely honed. Through watching the pilots closely, the team is learning how to stop overruns early, which should save money. These refined management processes will also allow us to drive out one month of our target three-month cycle time improvement that we discussed for product launch cycles.

Overall, Ray thinks the division is on schedule to go into the next fiscal year having recovered the cost of implementing the "being there" technologies and techniques. Sandra's team forecasts that by the end of the second year of using the new methods, product development cost will have declined by 6 to 7 percent. One month out of product development cycles will have been eliminated, and there will be no decline in quality or innovation.

"We're excited by these results," says Ray.

"Well, Chris," Marvin says, "looks like you have another group of converts. But that wasn't the complete list of our goals," he says, turning back to Ray.

"No, it wasn't," agrees Ray, and reiterates the original goals of the project: save 12 percent, take 90 days out of product cycle and raise revenue by getting closer to customers. "As you and I have discussed," says Ray, "we're ready to have the executive team look at product profitability and analyze the portfolio of projects in order to take out another 5 percent of development cost."

"Excellent," responds Marvin. "Let's start getting the portfolio meetings scheduled."

Ray says he'll get that done this week. Having finished the status report on his team's progress thus far, he addresses the next major phase of the project: examining the product development cycle and how it functions across departmental and corporate boundaries. "So far, we've been able to get our work done within product development, with only minor touch points outside the organization," Ray explains. But the product launch cycle involves additional spheres of influence—which extend across the company and eventually to suppliers, contractors and consultants.

Spheres of Influence

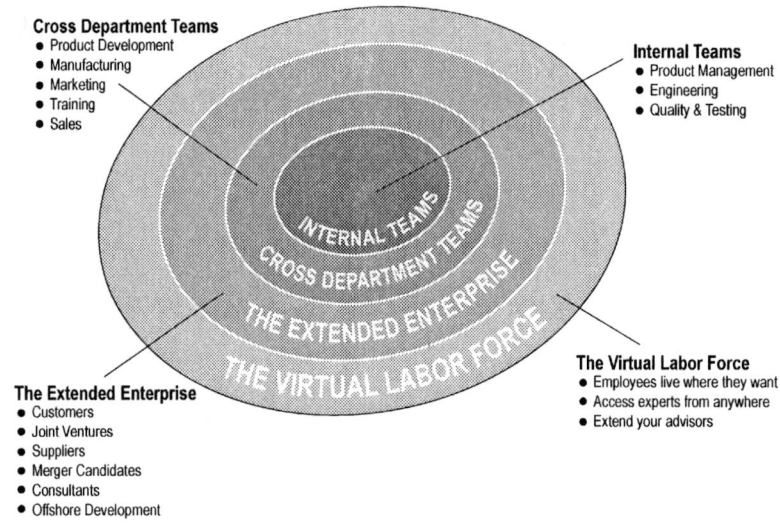

Ray, Sandra and Chris think there is another 2 to 3 percent of costs—and another 60 days out of the product development and launch cycle—to be saved by streamlining this process. The first step is working with various departments to address the activities that need to get done in parallel more effectively. "For instance, as we looked at the project you used as an example when we first talked about engaging Chris," Ray explains, "we found several problems that led to revenue being delayed by over 90 days."

- Coordination between design engineering and manufacturing engineering was strong, but small changes in the design schedule were not communicated effectively. This meant the loss of a few days at a stretch while the prototyping time needed in the factory was rescheduled. Delays in getting change orders for prototype parts turned around complicated matters further. Overall, small schedule slips between design engineering and the factory resulted in the loss of almost six weeks out of a 12-month project.
- Even worse, at one point in the project, a conservative master schedule showed an additional month's delay in engineering and manufacturing. Internal team leaders did a great job of making up that month, but that feat wasn't communicated to the marketing department, which was still relying on the master schedule. That gaffe resulted in marketing materials being more than a month late.
- Several suppliers were involved in producing parts for the early launch, but a change in suppliers wasn't communicated effectively to the purchasing and logistics division. That created a shortage of parts in the supply chain early on that kept factory lines from getting up to speed.

- Because of poor communication with the training department, there was insufficient time scheduled for product management to assist in developing the field sales and services training materials. When the product was ready to be launched, development and manufacturing were done, but the field wasn't ready to sell the product.

"So," concludes Ray, "even though we finished the design of the product essentially on schedule, we had an almost 90-day lapse in revenue. Our customers were expecting this new line, so revenue for the prior product release fell off, and the 90-day loss in revenue was significant."

The root cause of the problem, he explains, was planning and communication between teams. The project started with good schedules and plans for most of the teams, but it was difficult to keep all of the projects in sync as things changed. Several of the teams were in different cities, and some of the teams were in different countries. There were lots of conference calls to try to keep people on the same page—and the company even flew project managers into headquarters every two months to keep the project coordinated. "But a lot of things changed between meetings, and we were never able to completely freeze the schedule," sighs Ray.

Another flaw was that a lot of the managers had conservative buffers built into their schedules. As tasks were completed ahead of schedule in some areas, the teams were not able to accelerate the work in other areas to take advantage of the gains. So while slips caused the whole project to go backward, gains weren't harvested to bring it back forward. That, too, contributed to much of the 90-day slip.

"Sounds like a classic project management problem to me," says Marvin. "Who was the head project manager?"

That was part of the problem, Ray and Sandra explain. Each department had a project manager, but there wasn't really an overall leader for the launch of the product. Instead, there was a loosely connected set of projects run by different departments in different locations. Consequently, there was lot of miscommunication and lost productivity between teams. The marketing manager for the product was tasked with pulling everything together in the end, but he had a full-time job running his own team and the outside marketing consultants. He also didn't have the authority to direct changes on other teams. What was needed—and lacking—was a full-time program manager with the authority to make sure everything came together and the job got done.

"Why didn't we have someone like that?" Marvin asks.

Ray offers a few reasons:

- All of the department heads are very protective of their own work and their own resources. Naming a program manager for the entire launch and giving that manager the authority to direct teams in different departments would have cut across a lot of powerful boundaries.

- No one wanted to give up any of his or her department's head count to be responsible for pulling it all together. Leading the project would have been an extremely time-consuming job, and most people felt they were too busy to take on the task.
- The level of project management varied from department to department. Some departments worked from well-structured plans with critical paths, resource assignments and records of actual time spent and work left to complete. Other teams work from loosely compiled lists of tasks to be done, but didn't estimate the workload, much less consider ideas such as a critical path.
- The directors couldn't agree on the complete set of skills that were needed for a program manager. The company simply doesn't have a lot of employees who have a complete understanding of sales, field service, training, marketing, product management, manufacturing and logistics. Each department head would only allow his or her people to report to someone who understood their business area.
- Once we got the department heads to see that there really needed to be a launch manager, no one could agree to whom the launch manager should report. There was probably a lot of fear that the department that was responsible for product launch would become the greatest among equals—and that's not something people sign-off on readily.

"Wow," says Marvin. "So what do you recommend?"

Ray responds that he and Sandra decided to turn to Chris on this question. Chris then explains what he's learned from working with other clients. "Only a few companies do concurrent product development well," he explains, "and when they do, it's only on their largest projects. The techniques and talent to do so are simply too scarce at this point."

The good news, he says, is that the methods employed within the pilot projects are the baseline for working across departments. Basic things like planning, assigning and supervising work, storing work on the collaboration database and communicating constantly within and across teams remain necessities. "But as you implement these core skills across all of the departments involved in a product launch, there are a number of other things that you must get right," Chris says, and highlights the following:

- This is a substantial change to the way the company currently operates. The overall sponsor must be the senior executive so that when the program manager makes suggestions that cut across departments, he or she is operating with authority.
- The person who runs the product launch must have the influence to direct project managers from the various departments.
- While every project doesn't need to be run with the same level of detail, each project needs a plan, and the plans need to be linked together into a program plan.

- Visibility across projects in the project collaboration database is critical. Managers need to expose their problems and their contingency buffers and talk about the probability of dates moving both forward and backward so the overall program manager can take advantages of gains to make up for slips. This means that managers must be rewarded for allowing visibility and making changes for the good of the overall team.
- Deliverables from all projects need to be shared in the project collaboration database and maintained under version control so that as they are updated they are immediately available to other team members.
- There need to be frequent and formal walk-throughs scheduled using the Internet meeting software and including formal agendas to review deliverables, project status, issues and risks and opportunities to improve the results of the project.
- Escalation becomes critical, and it is important that escalation is viewed positively at each level of the company. People cannot be allowed to think that if they escalate a problem, they are putting their peers in another department on report. Cross-discipline problems can only be solved efficiently if problems are raised to the level where they are visible to someone who works across department boundaries to solve the problem.

"Do you expect to get resistance from the other departments?" Marvin asks.

Chris responds that there are two problems that will probably need to be addressed. First, the managers in other departments do not necessarily have project management and team member skills as a core competence. It will be more difficult for them to work in a distributed environment if both the project disciplines and the distributed team disciplines are new. Second, Chris and Sandra's team has had some conversations with people in other departments such as marketing and sales and gotten the sense that many people feel that adding process will stifle creativity.

"We need to help them understand that this process *channels* that creativity and helps them to have the strong financial impact that helps the company make money," he says.

The solution requires changes to organizational behavior, processes, and visibility through tools, Chris continues. It also requires that people collaborate and cooperate more effectively for the good of the program. All of this takes training so that there is a core competence of working together as a multi-discipline team in a single program, and a core competence in doing so across departments, distances and time zones—just as if it were done within the single organization of product development.

Organizationally, it is critical that the overall program managers are broadly skilled individuals who have more than one of the disciplines of their project team. They must be strong business leaders who can bring business judgment, not just program management skills, to the team.

They must be able to work in a matrix environment, where people from multiple departments are assigned to the project on a task-specific basis.

"Since no single person is strong at everything, it is important that you build teams with complementary rather than similar skills," Chris says. For example, if the overall program manager is a strong marketing and product management leader, then the leaders of the product management and marketing teams can be more junior and assigned to learn from the senior leader. But in that case, the manufacturing and engineering leaders must be very strong because those skills are not the core competence of the overall program leader. "That way you will build the total skill set necessary for a successful project in the team," he explains.

If it is a large program and the overall program manager has a business background rather than a program management background, then it is important to assign a well-trained project manager to work directly for the program manager to assist in project planning and project management disciplines. If it is a smaller project, then a business leader can usually apply a much less formal process to managing the project and may not need the project management assistance full-time.

The overall program manager should probably report to the department that has economic responsibility for product profit and loss. At Alpha Corp., that is generally the product marketing organization, Chris explains. Product marketing is responsible for making a plan to position a product for maximum profit impact, and then aligning the resources of the entire company to execute that plan.

"Finally," concludes Chris, "the project collaboration database becomes increasingly important because it is the location where projects are rolled up into programs, where cross-project dependencies are identified and tracked and where deliverables are stored so that everyone has access independent of organization, time zone or geography."

"Our processes for launching this program across our departmental boundaries are almost exactly the same as they were for launching the 'being there' tools and methods for the product development organization," adds Ray.

"However, if we're going to do this," Ray continues, "you must become the sponsor, Marvin. I'm prepared to offer Sandra as the overall program manager, but she must report to you for this program, and all of your direct reports need to understand and agree that this is an important initiative."

"Done," says Marvin.

Before concluding the meeting, Ray outlines the stickiest problems that Sandra will face under Marvin's sponsorship. Marvin then agrees that the following changes are critical and promises his buy-in:

1. A group of core advocates need to be identified and assigned to the program. This group will be the steering committee that signs off on new business practices and gets buy-in from the respective department heads and peers. The group will report its recommendations to Marvin and his direct reports on at least a monthly basis.
2. As in the product development pilots, the program needs to have well-documented business values. In the case that has been discussed, the goal was to contribute 2 to 3 percent in overall cost reduction in product development and product launch costs by shortening the product development cycle by approximately 60 days. For most new products, the impact of 60 days of incremental revenue far exceeds the impact of the cost savings.
3. The company must have clearly defined processes that cut across all divisions and are aimed at creating the economic values that have been identified. Since product management has the most formally documented processes, the combined project team will integrate the product launch business practices from manufacturing, marketing, sales and even finance. These practices needed to be well-taught at the same time the company teaches the new tools, just as was done when the "being there" program was launched within product development.
4. Since the company has already gained significant experience with the "being there" methods and tools, a pilot is not necessary. Until the new techniques and tools are common

across the entire company, programs will be selected based on the available impact.

"Marvin, we believe that the time to benefit will be even shorter than it was in product development, since we have the learning of that division to build upon," concludes Ray.

"Excellent. We'll make this the dominant subject of this week's senior management meeting, and I expect to find my direct reports very supportive of the concepts," says Marvin.

Chapter 13 Takeaways

When working across departments, the same basic "being there" methods apply. However, because of the complexities involved in a cross-departmental initiative, there are several additional keys to success:

1. The overall sponsor of the project must be a senior executive so that when suggestions to cut across departments are made, he or she is operating with authority.
2. The person who runs the project must have the influence to direct project managers from the various departments.
3. While not every project needs to be run with the same level of detail, each project needs a both a plan and a program plan.
4. Managers must be rewarded for creating visibility across projects in the project collaboration database.
5. Deliverables from all projects should be shared and constantly updated in the project collaboration database.
6. There must be frequent and formal walk-throughs scheduled using the Internet meeting software.
7. Escalation must be viewed positively at each level of the company. People cannot be allowed to think that if they escalate a problem, they are putting their peers in another department on report.

Chapter 14: Managing the Extended Enterprise

A few months later, Ray and Sandra meet with the executive management team of the entire division. Use of the new tools and techniques has been progressing well for the design and launch of several new products, as well as for the ongoing support of other product revisions. The company is rolling out the techniques through the remaining internal projects and is now ready to look at the extended enterprise, including the company's suppliers, contractors and customers.

Ray opens the meeting by passing out a brief document and giving people time to read it:

The Mars Orbiter: A $600 Million Failure

The way it is. From the official "Mars Climate Orbiter Failure Report":

The failure board's first report identifies eight contributing factors that led directly or indirectly to the loss of the [Mars Climate Orbiter]. These contributing causes include inadequate consideration of the entire mission and its post-launch operation as a total system, inconsistent communications and training within the project and lack of complete end-to-end verification of navigation software and related computer models. The "root cause" of the loss of the spacecraft was the failed translation of English units into metric units in a segment of ground-based, navigation-related mission software...

The report goes on to explain that the Mars Orbiter was built using extensive corporate and contractor support, with individual components, sub-assemblies, internal electronics and software coming from multiple vendors in the United States and Europe. The failure of the project could be traced back to one major cause: poor communication among teams. Part of the navigation software was built in English units and the other part in metric units.

The fact that the Orbiter was actually launched indicates that the teams did communicate on some level, the report says; however, the fact that the system was built using two sets of units and that the group was not able to overcome the consequent issues in additional testing show that the teams did not work in concert and with constant and rich communications. Instead, individual teams took ownership of parts of the software spec, built them and tested them, and then gave their pieces to NASA to assemble and test.

When everyone has finished reading, Ray says, "While none of our supplier integration failures are nearly this dramatic, can everyone think of at least a few examples in which a communication failure with our suppliers—or our customers—caused a serious failure?"

Several heads nod, and one executive actually chuckles out loud as he thinks about his own personal horror stories (and reflects thankfully, that for most companies, those stories do not get printed in the newspaper or brought up at engineering conferences in discussions of new ways to design best practices).

Ray passes out a second page of paper and says, "Each of your teams has had some significant experience with the 'being there' tools in efforts to improve communications within your departments and to cause richer communication among the division's cross-discipline teams. Now, before we look at how we could use these techniques to improve our own external relationships, let's think about how our new state of the possible could have changed the outcome of the Mars Orbiter."

The way it could have been. Ray's second piece of paper reads as follows:

NASA selects an Internet collaboration database site to host all of the projects related to the development and construction of the Mars Orbiter. Within the boundaries of security, teams that are working on related components have direct access to status, information and details on design from related projects, not just their own projects. The collaboration site, combined with Internet meeting software, enables teams and team members to share data and deliverables, record and monitor project risks and hold content-rich meetings between team leaders and the team members of remote teams. These individuals work hand in hand on the project despite geographic, time zone and corporate boundaries.

Very early in the project, teams working together note the difference in units of measure and record that as an issue and a risk that needs to be resolved in the critical path of project startup. Because the issue is identified early (due to rich integration walk-throughs), the first decision on the project is to work using a single unit of measure, either English or metric. Identifying that one simple issue and reaching that decision early saves the probe.

The document continues,

Even if the integration design meetings had not caused the issue to surface that early, at the very least, the various teams—working together and communicating frequently—would have identified the risk at some point and focused more attention on the potential risk of working in dual units. They could have shared design documents and source code, allowing each team to verify that its software not only worked, but also worked in conjunction with everyone else's. Finally, program management would not have closed the issue until extensive analysis to assure that the difference in units was properly tested in all of the software had been completed.

In sum: Many sets of engineers can either produce many separate results or one set of results with many sets of reviews and tests. The Mars Orbiter project would have been more successful if its engineers had done the latter.

As people look up, Ray resumes. "Our products are not as complex as a Mars landing device, but they are very complicated," he says. "Individual engineers at our suppliers have good ideas that we can use, but our engineers rarely get to talk to them except through a few leaders and through our purchasing specifications. Our customers have even better ideas about how to use our products and how to make them more effective, but our product managers and design engineers have only infrequent exposure to them because we cannot afford the time to send people to the field. Instead, our managers and engineers get their input from field service people, who are helpful, but a far from perfect filter. Consequently, we lose a lot of good ideas and frequently fail to get work done right on the first try. Sometimes the flaws are small and difficult to detect until we are in production. Then we spend a lot of money reworking things under difficult conditions and exceptional time pressures.

Ray continues by explaining that to complicate matters, Alpha Corp. is well into the process of acquiring several companies. As it goes through these acquisitions, the company will need to give a lot of thought to how it is going to do due diligence and manage the integrations—from the day it decides on a transaction to the day the acquired company is fully integrated into marketing, sales, product design and development processes. And, of course, each of the companies will come with its own set of customers, suppliers and partners, making the acquisitions even more complex.

Ray brings out the sphere of influence diagram that has been driving the program for the last several months and lets people study it before going on.

Spheres of Influence

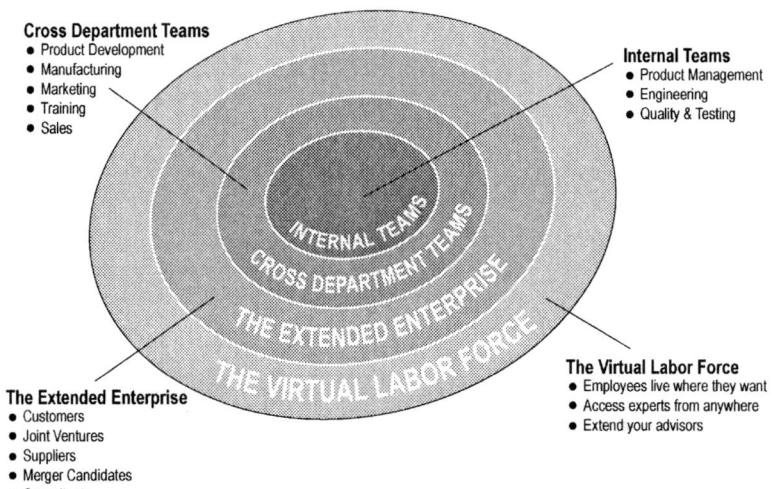

"Now that we are well into the change of our own company, it is time for us to address the third sphere of influence and begin to talk to our suppliers, joint ventures, merger candidates, offshore development contractors and, most important, our customers," Ray says.

He and the other leaders go on to agree that today's discussion will be successful if they can do the following:

- Discuss and agree on the objectives and measurable values for integration of suppliers and customers.
- Understand and approve the changes to the supporting technology.

- Discuss and agree on changes to business practices when they reach customers, partners, suppliers and contractors.
- Grasp the distinctive issues that are encountered in acquisitions and identify business practices that would help improve the timeframe and integration of those acquisitions.
- Understand the unique issues for the India development teams and how to make the teams a success for their division.

Marvin then says, "This is a great deal of detail for us to cover at the most senior level of the company. We are covering it here today because making changes that cut across the company, our suppliers and our customers will require me to be the overall sponsor. It will also require each of you to sponsor the changes in your departments, as well as with your customers, contractors and suppliers. I've asked Ray to assign Sandra to me full-time as the program manager for this change and for Ray to be the day-to-day sponsor of the program."

Measurable Objectives

Sandra takes over the meeting at this point and notes that, to date, the change management teams have done a good job of only changing things that will result in a solid economic return. The core team has agreed to recommend to management that the change to the business practices be designed to target the following objectives:

- A 30- to 45-day contribution to cycle time improvement on those projects with substantial contractor or supplier content. This would be done by starting projects faster, resolving problems earlier and faster and improving teamwork within the engineering teams, as well as by building inventory and manufacturing in the supply chain faster as new products come to market.

- A 3 to 4 percent cost reduction through two sources. First, by identifying and solving problems faster and more easily with partner suppliers, which would reduce the amount of engineering time spent on re-work. Second, by reducing the cost and lost time of travel for teams that are working with remote suppliers.
- An average of 2 to 3 percent increase in revenue per customer through improved customer satisfaction by having engineering personnel more accessible to customers to solicit their input on future product designs. Sandra notes that sales has signed up for this measurable goal.

In addition to these measurable improvements, the core team feels the company can get substantial additional but less measurable benefits in the integration of target acquisitions and winning major competitive deals, Sandra explains. The key to doing so is better leveraging the product management team with the sales team on the company's largest and most competitive deals.

Supporting Technologies

Sandra continues by explaining that the basic technologies that would be used to support the extended enterprise are the same tools they are all familiar with: Internet meeting software, project collaboration databases, instant messenger, Web cams, electronic whiteboards and tablet PCs to support engineers that do not have access to whiteboard technology.

"The fundamental difference to the technology," says Sandra, "is the amount of information that must reside outside the firewall, or flow through the firewall."

"Wait a minute," the CIO responds immediately. "This is our most secure product information. We can't put that outside the firewall, and we certainly can't poke holes in the firewall to move the information around. If we link our corporate computers to our suppliers and customers, we run the risk that hackers to the suppliers' or customers' computers can automatically get access to ours."

With Chris' help, Sandra explains that there are a number of hosted collaboration sites that provide secure Web sites for project collaboration databases and for Internet meeting centers. A hosted Internet meeting center allows people to run meetings exactly the same as they do inside their company with their customers and our suppliers. The meeting center technology runs on a separate computer that is used only by the teams and does not keep their files on its system. So, when a meeting ends, the information that was being shared is no longer on the hosted site.

The project collaboration database would need to be on a very secure site, a place where the company is willing to put information that it would share with its partners, she says. The core team anticipated this when starting the original project and therefore selected a vendor that provided hosted services. Projects can be run as a combination of "internal projects," which occur behind the company's firewall or on a separate hosted system that is accessible only to employees of the company, and "shared projects" that run on the hosted services computer accessible to the partner's teams and all members of the internal teams.

"It turns out that most of the information we share with our partners is about specifications for subcomponents and specifications for interfaces," Sandra says. "That is not the most secure information in the company. So we should keep the information that is most secure, like patents, designs and schedules for new products' market launch plans on the corporate systems, while we keep less secure information on the shared site, where it will be accessible to the customers and suppliers that have the security to access to it. By the way, several of our competitors run their entire corporate system hosted, and they are completely comfortable with the security arrangements, but we don't need to go that far right away if we're not ready to."

Next Sandra explains that there are other reasons for keeping environments for internal management separate from the shared environments with customers and suppliers. For example, her teams frequently put information in their issues and risks system about the issues that they are encountering with a specific customer or supplier. They don't always want to share that information with the customer or supplier because they would not be able to be candid about the problems and potential resolutions if they thought the customer or partner might be able to see it. That type of information should also be in the internal corporate system, she says.

"So," Sandra says, "teaching our managers what to put in the shared environment and what to protect in our proprietary systems is a critical training issue, but we are confident that we can provide the appropriate balance of security and access to make collaboration work with our most important partners, whether they are joint ventures, suppliers or customers."

Business Practices
"That brings us to our discussion of business practices and how we need to train our teams, suppliers and customers to make them effective users of our 'being there' technologies and processes," Sandra resumes.

"We've already discussed the first major point," she says. "We need to be very sure that we have a secure environment for our own highly secure internal information and a more accessible environment for shared information. Our professionals and managers must be trained to think carefully about what information can be shared outside the company so that they do not post secure or sensitive information to the shared environment."

She then explains that team leaders and team members from suppliers and partners will need to be trained on the same processes that are used internally. Having developed good training programs inside the company, Alpha Corp. will then need to make those training programs available to partners—and expect those partners to make the investment in training people who will be part of their core project teams. Sandra then flashes up a set of the core processes and explains those that would be critical for running teams across corporate boundaries, grouped into basic project skills and those skills for managing across boundaries.

Basic Project Skills

Project & Program Planning and Portfolio Reporting. With partners and customers it is especially important to be competent at defining projects of any size. When programs work across corporate boundaries, the team encounters the unique problem of creating well-defined programs that are made up of projects that are executed separately and brought together at key touch points. For example, as a supplier creates a subsystem, it becomes a separate project run at the supplier's site, but one that exists within an overall program to ship the final product. Program plans, milestones, critical path dependencies and key technical integration points need to be carefully identified, agreed upon and shared across teams in the project collaboration environment.

Project Startup, Brainstorming and Execution. Partners need to be taught lessons learned internally about what work should be done without traveling and when a team should be brought into one place.

Constant, well-structured and rich communication is a requirement for a successful venture that cuts across both geographic and corporate boundaries. The enabling technologies of Internet meeting software and electronic whiteboards are as important here as in internal projects. However, it is critical to build trust across teams, so bringing the teams together periodically to brainstorm and solve intuitive problems is an important concept to be reinforced with the partners. The biggest challenge with customers is to convince them that all work does not need to be done on the customer's site.

Assigning and Supervising Work for People at Remote Sites. Most of the time, work is assigned to a supplier for a total project, so there is less emphasis on assigning and supervising work to individuals in other companies. But occasionally, a team uses contractors and suppliers to perform task work within the team, or Alpha Corporation's employees perform work as team members on supplier projects. Assigning and supervising tasks to remote personnel is a core competence, one that is further complicated by the fact that the employee works for a different company, causing a lack of clarity about who has the authority to assign and supervise work. When that situation exists, it needs to be managed carefully, with an emphasis on building trust and getting authority from the partner or customer to allow the leader of a team to supervise employees. The techniques are the same as assigning work to our own employees, but the sensitivities are very different.

Managing Across Boundaries

Walk-throughs. A key to rich and structured communication is scheduling and conducting regular walk-throughs on plans, status and deliverables across corporate boundaries to keep teams on the same page. The Internet meeting software and the walk-through disciplines that Alpha Corp. has developed will make this work. Sandra's team has developed a core competence on running successful meetings and walk-throughs whether together or remote.

"We will need to carefully structure communications to teach those habits to the partners,' Sandra says. "It seems silly, but everyone in our organization now starts meetings with the phrase, 'This meeting will be successful if…' We need to get our partners to adopt that same simple principle. Remember that it took us three to four months to get comfortable running remote meetings. It will take as long for our partners, who are doing this for the first time."

Quality Assurance Across Organizational Boundaries. Quality assurance is just another deliverable and another work process. However, the Mars Orbiter project demonstrates that testing at the interfaces of products and across an entire system made up of subcomponents is one of the most important issues the company faces. Alpha Corp. will need to develop excellent cross-discipline test processes, store them in the collaboration database and walk through them on the Internet meeting software. Fortunately, the new collaboration environment allows people to assemble a quality assurance team that cuts across the core team and its suppliers, sometimes reaching all the way to the customer. Having a single test team that cuts across all of the organizations avoids the conflict that arises when someone finds something wrong with another organization's work product.

"We need to get people to understand that it is a single product made up of many parts, and that we are successful when the end product works and can be manufactured reliably and inexpensively," Sandra says. "It is not sufficient to believe that it is OK when one individual team's components work."

Product Launch. For the most part, Alpha Corp. is the integrator that sells and ships the final assemblies. But its products are differentiated by the content and components that its gets from its suppliers. "We lose a major advantage if we do not manage our product launch programs to embody the messages from our suppliers as well as our own," Sandra says. "Also, we generally lose a month or more getting the final designs and manufacturing processes nailed down and getting the supply chain filled." Those roles cut across companies, organizations within companies and geographies, so Alpha Corp. needs to get all of the departments and suppliers on a single page to avoid the slips that occurred toward the end of the last few product launches. A well-structured program under a single program manager will enable cross-discipline teams from multiple companies to operate in a single product launch, with coordinated engineering, marketing, manufacturing and supply chains.

Continuous Interaction With the Factory. The company will need to stay as connected with the supplier's factories as it is with its own. This will mean getting suppliers to embrace the technologies and changes all the way to their factories, so that joint engineering teams can take time and cost out of the test and problem solving cycles.

Solving Problems With New Products at the Customer Site. Finally, the company can improve its responsiveness to customers by bringing a problem-solving team together from both the company and its partners and suppliers to address issues as they arise. Doing so requires an excellent view of the problem that is being addressed (and is stored on the collaboration database). It then requires regular and rich communication across meeting managers to build response teams from the company that are supported by the suppliers, with only the smallest and most critical parts of the team physically on site.

Next, Sandra explains that the company has well-documented procedures on each of these processes from work done inside the company. So, as it brings each supplier or customer into the distributed processes, the company will need to decide whether to use the company's processes or the partner's processes. Then it can document and teach the processes and arrange for regular reviews to make sure that when problems occur, both the root cause and the immediate problem are solved.

Generally, a supplier should use the company's processes unless the supplier has a best practice that is more effective, she says. If a supplier does have a more effective best practice, then the company should adopt that as part of its core processes. What is most important is that the processes are well-documented and shared across supplier and company teams. Standard processes can be stored as templates in the project collaboration database and used as a point of departure on each new project. That way, each team will learn what works and what does not, continuously improving the communication and work product of the company's teams as well as the suppliers.

Sandra stops and asks, "Does this make sense so far? Are there any processes that we have missed? Will we be able to make this kind of change with our suppliers?"

After a great deal of discussion, the group agrees that they will be able to manage their supplier relationships this way and see how doing so could produce the target benefits.

"Excellent," says Sandra. "Now, with our customers we have a more significant issue, because we can't mandate processes the way we can with suppliers. So we will need to help our customers understand the value of our processes in terms of cost, time and quality in ways that are economically important to them, not just to us. The good news is that as we've developed these processes within our own company, we've included a few customers and suppliers and have documented the economic value at each step. Consequently, we have good case studies and have developed some enthusiastic supporters that we can leverage as we go to the rest with requests for change."

In sum, says Sandra, the keys to successful business practices are:
- Having well-understood processes and tying those processes to economic benefits for the customer and the supplier
- Having technology available outside the company's firewall and having confidence in the security of information stored there
- Making that information accessible to people who have the need to know independent of geography and corporate boundaries
- Training managers and team members on both the processes and what information should be communicated and what information should still be held in the company's internal systems
- Bringing the teams together on regular intervals to develop trust and to brainstorm

She and her team have decided that the new processes will work best for mid-size and longer projects at first. Then, as people get comfortable with the technology and the state of the possible, they can be adapted to even the smallest assignments.

As Sandra comes to her last discussion slide, Ray stops and asks, "How are we doing with our meeting objectives so far? He puts the meeting objectives slide back up and confirms that the team has successfully completed the first three: discuss and agree on objectives and measurable values for integration of suppliers and customers; understand and approve changes to the supporting technology; and discuss and agree on the changes to the business practices when it reaches customers, partners, suppliers and contractors.

Chapter 14 Takeaways

Applying the 'being there' tools and techniques to suppliers and customers ca produce real measurable value. Ray and Sandra are managing toward:

- Improvement in time to market by starting projects faster and resolving problems as they come up without having to wait for supplier meetings
- Real cost savings through reduced travel, better design with suppliers and better customer input on products
- Increased revenue per customer by soliciting regular input from customers and engaging customer leadership in product planning and product design
- Increased sales wins by using product management more effectively to support the field without travel

The keys to achieving these successes are as follows:

- Having program sponsorship by the most senior executives in the company
- Having well-understood processes and tying those processes to economic benefits for the customer and the supplier
- Having technology available outside the company's firewall and having confidence in the security of the information stored there
- Making that information accessible to people who have the need to know independent of geographic and corporate boundaries

- Training managers and team members on both the processes and on what information should be communicated and what information should remain in the company's internal systems
- Bringing the teams together on regular intervals to develop trust and to brainstorm

Chapter 15:
Mergers and Acquisitions & Offshore Development

After a short break, the group reconvenes to discuss mergers and acquisitions and the use of India software development teams. Ray explains that mergers are distinctive situations because they involve all of the sensitivities of a team that has just been acquired. Team members want to retain their own autonomy and yet be thought of as a valuable part of the new, larger team. India software development is particularly unique because it taps into a huge talent pool that is available for about one-third of the cost of talent in company's core development centers.

India Software Development

However, India software development comes with two specific problems: First, while most of the Indian software developers speak English, their vocabulary, slang and culture are very different, creating communication issues. Second, the time zone shifts between the United States and India are radical. Oftentimes, there are no hours of normal work overlap. So while the payoff of Indian software development is enormous, communication is particularly hard to establish.

Mergers & Acquisitions

With Chris' help, Ray explains that mergers and acquisitions are not unlike the customer scenario discussed earlier. The objective with M&A is to improve working relationships, to develop common technologies and processes and to move to fully integrated teams as quickly as possible. M&A is more like the customer scenario than the supplier scenario because there are tremendous sensitivities in implementing change with the acquired team.

"As Marvin has said," Ray adds, "we can direct the change as a function of the acquisition, but it is far more important that we sell the change and have it embraced enthusiastically." He goes on to explain that the hosted sites that the company uses to work with customers and suppliers are particularly useful early in M&A activity, before the organizations are allowed to co-mingle their operational systems. Because the hosted shared systems are independent enough to be used with customers and suppliers, it's fine to use them to do shared work during the M&A activity.

The core team has identified several ways that the company can use the new tools and processes to make both the merger process and post-merger integration more successful. First, during the merger negotiations and contracting, it can engage a number of third parties and create a large number of documents under substantial time pressure. The project collaboration database can be used to store a set of milestones and deliverables for attorneys, accountants and management. The issues and risks tracking systems allow people to identify open issues that must be resolved, assign those issues and track them to make sure that the company does not get to contract-signing day and find that several items have not been covered. Finally, the document management environment allows the company to store and track versions of the contracts and due diligence documents as they are assembled. As the documents are complete, the various parties can see the final versions and sign off on them.

"Contrast that type of control to the hundreds of emails that usually go back and forth. We waste hundreds of thousands of dollars keeping track of all the professional work that is being done by their internal and external accountants and lawyers as well as ours. Then when it comes time to finish the transaction, we sort through all of those documents and copies. Is it any surprise that we can never understand why the accounting and legal fees for mergers are always higher than we expected?" says Ray.

He continues, "At the same time that the finance and legal people are constructing the deal, the business people are building the business plan and looking for ways to streamline the business operationally." By using the project collaboration environment, they can keep a very good plan, compare business practices and develop a set of post-merger plans and practices that will achieve the goals of the merger. Equally important, each project has a well-defined project charter that lets the integration team understand what top management expects in terms of business value. "If there is no measurable value, there should be no project," Ray says.

By using the Internet meeting manager for working sessions, the company is able to put a small team on site at the acquisition and draw on a variety of experts at headquarters and around the world, he explains. That creates several tangible benefits, including lower travel costs, access to experts that otherwise could not be used and better use of the time of our internal and external personnel.

"We think this will yield substantial cost savings on each merger," Sandra adds, "but we don't have the benchmarks to compare like we do in product release, so it's much more difficult to quantify the benefits and make them economic values. If we do a good job of understanding our costs and our processes with the next acquisition, then we might be able to quantify the economic values for future acquisitions."

Finally, Ray explains that after an acquisition is complete, the M&A group has two major objectives. First, it needs to get the businesses working together effectively as quickly as possible. Second, it needs to merge the cultures and create a single business unit that can build and ship products as an integral unit. The company can do the business integration in two steps by getting teams that are developing products, sales plans and marketing materials together to work on the project collaboration database that is external for suppliers and customers.

"We can be up on that within days and working more effectively as a team from that point," Ray says. "Then, as the business is integrated over time, the next step is to bring the acquired company into our internal project collaboration database and begin to share resources and better manage the business overall. Each step generates real business integration value."

However, Ray says that the main benefit will occur when the Internet meeting manager is used to run collaborative meetings throughout the company. When that happens, Alpha Corp. will be able to put managers on site at the acquired company and still have them working with teams at its locations. Doing so opens a whole new range of managers to be part of the integration team. At the same time, Alpha Corp. can begin to staff projects without a lot of consideration to location, just as it did when it started working across our own engineering centers.

"But as we do this, we need to remember the diagram that we have used to guide our processes internally," notes Ray.

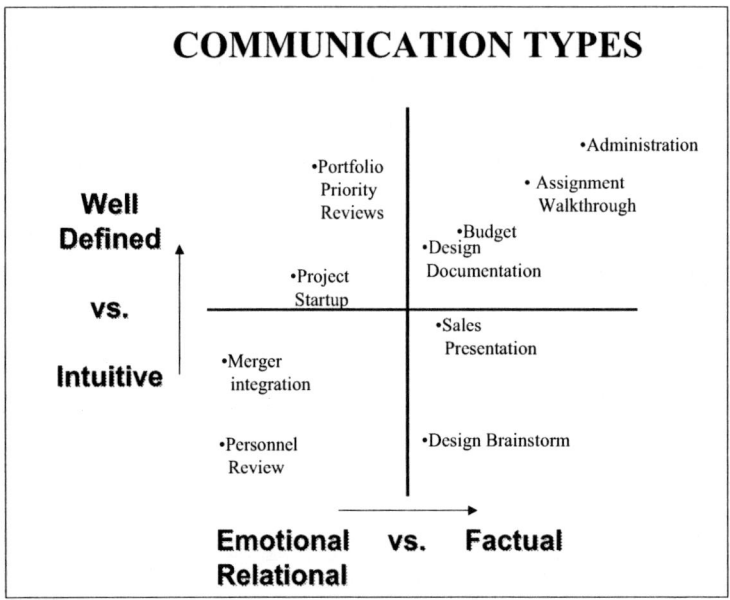

Ray then notes that a tremendous amount of the work that is done in early M&A integration is intuitive and is about building relationships and trust. Consequently, M&A is located very much in the lower left corner of the diagram. To achieve M&A success, managers need to manage by walking around and working with the new people.

Therefore, tools like Internet meeting manager are better for allowing managers to stay in touch with their old business while they go on site with a new business and build relationships that will enable them to do the tough integration tasks. Once the new business is running smoothly, the balance of travel can go back to 50/50 (50 percent at the old location and 50 percent at the new one), and then the occasional visit to the new location. The project collaboration tools allow managers to run an extended enterprise by being at the location with the greatest need for presence, but still being in touch with and able to run all the other businesses in the extended enterprise.

Marvin then asks, "Are we ready to use this on our next acquisition, which should happen within the next few weeks?" He explains that the head of M&A has expressed some concern because new technologies and processes are being thrust into the middle of a sensitive negotiation. However, the head of M&A has agreed to try the new processes if they are monitored carefully.

Marvin brings up a final topic by looking at his CIO and Ray and saying, "I know that we have made gains in using our software development labs in India, but it seems to me that we have genuinely under-utilized this function there. We give them special projects or a series of less important and less critical projects, and then discuss why we get less value from this operation than we should. I am looking forward to a presentation from the two of you on how we are going to leverage our recent successes to make India development and testing an important part of our future."

Ray looks at the CIO and says, "We have heard that message loud and clear. We think that you will be pleased with our progress and the lessons we have learned that will allow us to expand this capability."

"Great," says Marvin. "For now, our discussion applies only to information technology and engineering. Let's save that presentation for the end of the day, when we can let everyone else go."

Marvin, Chris, Ray and his team gather again later that day in Marvin's conference room. Chris opens the conversation by saying, "Isn't it curious that we call it *offshore development?* What does offshore development mean for a global company with engineers and manufacturing centers in a dozen countries, and sales and marketing efforts in most major world markets?" He then notes that the term offshore development evolved from U.S. companies that used low labor cost markets such as India, Mexico and the Philippines to develop software and to perform manufacturing functions.

Ray then explains that the team has looked extensively at the company's use of offshore development. It has studied Marvin's previous division and a number of Chris' most successful clients, as well as clients that have not yet achieved success. Ray has also spent more time with Li at IMT. He explains that India is the most widely used offshore development market because it has a good infrastructure, many companies that specialize in software development for U.S. enterprise, a broad population of well-trained software engineers and a very low cost per head for highly qualified engineers.

The companies the team has studied run a broad spectrum from those that use offshore development for simple tasks such as reporting and maintenance of legacy systems to those that use it for more sophisticated tasks such as regression testing and developing core products. The most sophisticated shops are beginning to push the envelope on 24/7 software development and software support, in which teams of engineers share problems around the clock. The two best examples the team has seen are a company that is developing software in the United States and Europe and running regression testing in India, and a company that is troubleshooting production problems for its support environment by passing the problem from European engineers to U.S. engineers to engineers in India in a true "follow the sun" support environment.

Ray continues, "We found that there are several characteristics that teams in the most successful shops share."

1. Team continuity
2. Top-down commitment
3. Measurable goals
4. A strong technology infrastructure
5. Well-understood and well-documented processes, particularly for assigning and supervising work
6. Well-trained teams

7. A walk-before-you-run (but by all means plan to run) approach to building success over time
8. Strong working relationships that are generally developed by spending time together in the formative stages and periodically refreshing the relationship through personal contact
9. Persistence with a discipline of identifying and working through problems, rather than falling back to the way things were done in the past
10. The ability to measure and continuously improve performance through processes, technology and training

"How are these 10 points any different than what we have done so far within the company and with our suppliers?" Marvin asks.

"In fact, it's not different at all," replies Ray. He explains that they will need to apply the same disciplines and the technologies that have already been mastered within the company to offshore development. Offshore development is a special situation in that there are tremendous economies to be gained due to differences in labor costs, but there are several unique conditions that must be overcome to achieve those economies. For example:

- Many people, including Alpha Corp.'s employees, have a built-up resistance to offshore development because they tried it when the technology and processes were not mature and determined

- that it was not productive. It is difficult to overcome those feelings.
- The teams in offshore development have almost no overlap in working hours, so collaboration and supervision of tasks require some new ways of thinking. Many teams fall back on using offshore teams for tasks that require minimal collaboration and supervision but provide the weakest returns.
- The end product is software and intellectual property, which is continuously changing rather than something physical that is manufactured. Offshore development is very different from offshore manufacturing; with the latter, once you have solved all of the problems, you are able to perform long repetitive runs of a product.
- While English is the common language for engineering in India, the United Kingdom and the United States, there are great differences in vocabulary and colloquialisms. For example, one of Alpha Corp.'s engineers was talking about a test bench for automotive parts that was shipped to India for repetitive testing of embedded software. The English instruction for starting the engine said, "Insert key and crank." The Indian test engineer, who had never driven a car, had no idea what the instructions meant and could not get in touch with his U.S. counterpart to get clarification. He spent most of the day trying to figure out what a crank was.

"For a repetitive process like testing, losing a day is disappointing," Ray notes, "but there are still substantial economies to be gained." Regression testing could be run like a factory for months and years based upon a set of well-defined test scenarios that are frequently updated, but rarely redesigned in entirety, he explains. When engineers are working together to design and build new intellectual property, those small communication errors can leak away a substantial percentage of gains in cost through lost productivity.

"That's interesting," says Marvin. "So how do you overcome those communication errors and productivity leaks?"

"That's where our list of offshore principles comes in," Ray replies. He then explains the 10 basic principles that Chris and his team have synthesized from their interviews with companies and team leaders that are successful, as well as from those who are not.

Team Continuity

Ray explains that the most important factor in the success of offshore development is team continuity. In cases where companies succeeded, they put together a team for a long-term project or a series of projects, and then left the team together with the same level of moderate turnover found in teams at a single location. The teams had structure, strong team leaders and the shared vocabulary that exists on all teams that have worked together for quite some time. They were able to communicate efficiently and with minimal misunderstandings because they interacted so regularly and understood each other well.

By contrast, companies that regarded the teams as interchangeable parts to be assembled and reconfigured regularly based on immediate demand found that the cost of miscommunication often sapped all of the cost savings of offshore development. It also built up a high sense of frustration. In such situations, companies would only stay with offshore developers when they forced to by top management.

Companies with large information technology or software product development shops that assembled teams that built, tested and maintained software over time had the ability to sustain continuity and to achieve the economies of offshore development. Similarly, consulting companies that developed teams made up of consultants that went to the customer's site and then worked with a consistent set of India developers brought tremendous value in cost savings and time to market. By contrast, companies that regarded programmers in India as interchangeable, peak-capacity programmers that could be swapped in and out often found that the difficulties of communication and coordination were too great to gain any substantive benefits.

Top-Down Commitment
Chris reminds Marvin that, as everyone in the room knows, top-down commitment is critical to any major behavioral change. Everything about the "being there" approach has been successful to this point because of

continuous involvement and commitment from the senior executives, he says. This has included their willingness to invest in the processes and temporarily lose productivity in order to reap long-term benefits.

"No change you have implemented is more substantial that this one in terms of changing the way people think and believe," Chris says. He and the others then discuss techniques that can be used to solidify this kind of top-down commitment:

- Visible participation and leadership from senior executives
- Showing engineering leaders and project managers the economic benefits of engaging offshore development rather than continuing to build increasingly larger teams on the core development campuses
- Setting management objectives for offshore content and rewarding teams for making the new approaches work successfully, first through demonstrated milestones and then through demonstrated economic gains (by doing the same work as in the past at the same level of effort with much less expensive employees)
- Creating work environments for employees that moderate some of the time zone issues: allowing employees to create flexible work schedules that overlap with their Indian counterparts or, even better, giving people the technology to work at home, which allows them to view working with their Indian counterparts as a benefit. For example, putting high-speed

communications lines and a second phone line into an engineer's home allows her to work with the India contractors from a home office. She can get up early, work with colleagues in India and then have breakfast with her family before coming to the office around mid-morning. Or similarly, she can leave the office early, coach a child's athletic team, have dinner with the family and then pick up work in the early evening, when her counterparts in India are at work during their morning.

Measurable Goals

The core team has established realistic measurable goals as the basis for everything it's done so far with the "being there" methodology, Ray says. Measurable economic goals for offshore development derive from two principles:

1. **Cost.** Labor and facilities in markets such as India are roughly 20 to 30 percent of the cost of comparable talent in markets such as San Francisco, London and Boston. Companies that open their own development centers in India or similar markets will characteristically see a cost-per-hour reduction of 65 to 75 percent. Even the use of a development subcontractor who makes a reasonable profit allows a savings of 60 to 65 percent. This works out to roughly two and a half to three engineers for the price of one.
2. **Time.** By effectively tying into the 24-hour clock, it is possible to work on projects 16 to 18 hours a day rather than 8 to 10

hours a day. Some tasks are accelerated nicely by having extra time. Companies can, for example, develop all day and regression-test all night. Or they can work around the clock to fix a critical problem in a customer's production software.

It is unrealistic to expect that the company will gain those kinds of benefits during startup, notes Ray. In fact, it should expect extra costs as it develops new processes and procedures, communication styles and trust between teams. Therefore, the core team has set milestones every 90 days: It expects to invest 10 to 15 percent extra for the first 90 days, break even for the next 90 days and then get to the point where it is two-thirds as productive in India at one-third the usual cost within 180 days. At this point, the changes should begin to yield substantial payback. Ideally, the engineers will be working seamlessly by the end of the first year, yielding a 65 percent savings for every engineer employed in India.

"We believe that having half of our development talent in India is the maximum mix that we can manage, at least for the next few years," Ray concludes.

Strong Technology Infrastructure
"Interestingly, other than what we've already implemented for our 'being there' program throughout the company, there is no additional technology required to do offshore development," Sandra says. She explains that the cornerstone technologies for offshore development are the project collaboration environment and Internet meeting software.

Also, the India contractors will need to have access to the source code library management systems and the test servers. That will allow the team to keep everything it needs in one place, organized and secure yet available to every member of the team. The Internet meeting software will allow leaders to assign and supervise work remotely and conduct structured walkthroughs to identify and solve problems. "Those are the essential communication tasks that are critical to making a team productive in multiple locations," Sandra says.

She also explains that the most important technology infrastructure change in offshore development is putting high-speed lines and additional telephone lines into the homes of engineers that work with both India and U.S. offices. These engineers need full access to the project collaboration environment and the Internet meeting software in order to do structured walkthroughs from home and deal with the time zone shifts.

Well-Understood and Well-Documented Processes
The most successful teams have well-documented and well-understood processes, Sandra says. One company her core team studied ran a particularly interesting and successful exercise: It brought leaders from India into a conference room in London together with the engineers they were going to support. The first step was to train all of the team members on the documented processes and make subtle changes to standard methods in order to make offshore development work effectively.

Once the leaders agreed to the processes, the London team members went back to their desks and the India team members stayed in the conference room. The project manager explained to everyone that the conference room door was about 5,000 miles and six time zones wide and that it would cost the team about $6,000 in travel costs and two to three work days each time it opened the door (equivalent to flying to London from India). Therefore, it was OK to open the door to fix process and communication problems, but the team needed to use collaboration tools to work on deliverables. After the project started (with everyone still in London), team members had daily meetings to talk about what was and wasn't working.

Once things were running smoothly, the team inserted an artificial five-time-zone shift between work hours, with team members from India coming in earlier and leaving earlier, exactly as they would when they went back to their own office. Again, they only opened the conference room door to meet with their London colleagues in order to work on processes and communication problems or for the occasional opportunity to socialize and build a sense of team.

After six weeks, the India team returned to its office. The combined team worked seamlessly for several years based on the well-understood processes, communication and the sense of trust that had been built during those first six weeks.

Sandra says her team has developed a well-defined set of software development processes, project management methods and supervision techniques, including structured walkthroughs at the beginning and end of each assignment. "These should serve us well for developing software," she says. The "being there" methods that had been developed for general management and communication would need almost no modification for use in offshore development. Soon, the company would bring the team leaders from India to the home office for a six-week training and indoctrination process like the one just described—subject to Marvin's approval in today's meeting.

Well-Trained Teams

She continued to explain that the conference room exercise was the baseline for training the remaining team members, but that it would not be necessary to conduct a six-week indoctrination for each member assigned to the team. Instead they would conduct up to two weeks of training during the first year for all team members. This training would include the basic software development methodologies, the "being there" methods and user training on the five basic technologies that were core to the offshore development environment.

New team members added after initial training would be given two weeks of training on the same techniques during their first year of employment on the team. Members from other departments that were assigned to work with product development would usually get an abbreviated training ranging from two days for executives to a week for active team members. The training would include mentorship by a product development team member.

"Training is particularly important for our professionals in any situation," adds Ray. "In the case of a major change such as adopting offshore development with minimal team travel, we feel it's critical to make the investment in training to avoid difficulties and frustration. This is a key demonstration of top-down commitment to program."

Walk Before You Run, but by All Means Plan to Run
"We've already established that repetitive or simple tasks are the easiest to do first, as the team is developing the trust and communication skills to do more sophisticated work like offshore development of a complex application," Chris says. He explains that walking before you run means initially doing the easiest, or least time-sensitive tasks, at the offshore development center and then extending its capabilities to more sophisticated work. The core team found several examples of these less complex tasks:

- Maintenance and bug-fixing of existing systems
- Regression testing, which, if done right, is highly repetitive and follows well -defined scripts
- New development of unsophisticated applications, such as straightforward reports and simple single-function programs

As team members developed trust and the knowledge of the total complex application being developed, the offshore members were able to take on the full capabilities of the core developers and work on any part of the application.

"It's important to remember that the developers in India are motivated by the same career challenges and goals that motivate software engineers everywhere," notes Chris. "They want to work on more challenging assignments, grow professionally and lead teams and ultimately perhaps become design leaders and see their ideas incorporated in systems and products." He explains that in those cases in which offshore developers were used as "excess capacity," they did not grow professionally, and companies were forced to rotate staff to give them richer assignments and retain top talent. Consequently, project teams that did not challenge their offshore developers not only failed to retain and motivate the best talent, they also failed to achieve the high level of productivity and cost benefit that was the main objective.

"So basically, while it's important to start with basic and repetitive tasks, it's equally important to regard remote or offshore developers as full team members and to give them a mix of challenging assignments that allow them to grow and mature over time—exactly as you would with any engineer in a headquarters location," Chris says.

Travel to Establish Strong Working Relationships
Chris then talks about one of the company's most successful customers. "We noted an interesting phenomena that existed in one of the company's groups," he says. The group was particularly tight-knit and

tended to reject the work of anyone who was not a member of the group, he explains. "We found several examples in which people had been viewed as poor performers until they came on site and developed a working relationship," he says. "Then they were viewed as extremely strong performers." Even after they went back to working in their home office, they retained the reputation of being strong performers and remained members of the extended team.

Although this is an extreme example, Chris notes, it highlights the fact that people work best with other people after they have developed a working relationship in person. While it's not possible to have every team member spend a month or two working on site with the home office team, it's important that key people (team leaders, managers and specialists) have the opportunity to work in a structured environment with the rest of the team. "However, you need to avoid falling into the field-trip trap," Chris says, "because then teams do not have the opportunity to build working relationships and trust. The key is to balance expense and productivity."

Persistence in Identifying and Solving Problems
Sandra explains that the conference room exercise is a first step in formalizing processes and solving problems rather than giving up. "It's important to know—and to demonstrate to the entire team—that the India team is made up of strong personnel who are of the same or greater capabilities as the on-site team," she says.

After assembling a strong team and developing well-documented processes, it's important to identify and document issues, develop resolution plans and work through problems, she says. The project collaboration environment contains an issues management system that can be used to document issues and resolution plans and then track those resolutions. "This gets the team beyond emotional issues and working on fact-based resolution of working problems," Sandra says.

Measure and Continuously Improve

Ray finishes the discussion by summarizing the basic measures of success for the company's offshore development in India. The stated goal is to achieve a 50 percent reduction in cost for all work that could be sent to India within a 12-month process, he says. If as much as 50 percent of the work can be outsourced to India, a 25 percent reduction in the total cost of software development could be achieved. This would be nearly a 4 percent reduction in the overall product development budget (given that much of the company's engineering does not involve software). To achieve that level of performance, the company will need to measure and improve the following key indicators:

- **Head count** in India versus the core engineering campuses to get to the 50 percent mix without increasing overall head count. This is likely to result in some reduction of head count in the core development teams. "It is much more palatable to take on this level of change during a period of head count growth or significant turnover," Ray says, "but this is an important way for the company to reduce cost during tough times."

- **Productivity** on basic tasks, which will get somewhat worse during startup. At the end of 90 days, a task that could have been done exclusively at one campus will take somewhat longer to complete with work done in India. "But it should be at the point where cost is break-even because the labor cost is lower," Ray says. Within a year, the team should be working seamlessly such that any task should take the same number of man hours, whether it is performed in India or at the core engineering site, or both.
- **Quality and rework,** which should be the same for work done in India as it is for work done at the core engineering campus. There should be no penalty in testing or integration for work done at two campuses.
- **Staff turnover and professional growth,** which should also be the same in India as it is at the core engineering site (and within acceptable norms). There will be some increase in turnover as the program is rolled out and some people choose to not participate or are ineffective, Ray explains, but once that settles out of the system, turnover should be the same as any other operation in the business.
- **Cost,** which should improve by 25 percent on total software development. Alternatively, there should be a 25 percent increase in development output that can be measured in revenue.

Ray then presents an overall business plan that shows a 15 percent increase in first-quarter costs and a 10 percent reduction in costs over the course of the year. "If this plan is acceptable, we'll execute the contracts and begin implementing the plan next month."

"This is a well-thought-out plan," Marvin responds. I'm delighted with the progress that we've made on the entire program and expect this to be the next major step."

Chapter 15 Takeaways

In studying the company's use of offshore development, Sandra's team looked at both successful and unsuccessful clients. The teams that were most successful shared the following 10 characteristics:

1. Team continuity
2. Top-down commitment
3. Measurable goals
4. A strong technology infrastructure
5. Well-understood and well-documented processes
6. Well-trained teams
7. A walk-before-you-run approach to building success over time
8. Travel to develop strong working relationships
9. Persistence in identifying and working through problems, rather than falling back on the way things were done in the past
10. The ability to measure and continuously improve performance

Chapter 16:

In Summary: How Virtual Should You Be?

By the end of 15 to 18 months, the operating modes that Ray's teams have adopted have become second nature and generated about 8 percent of the 12 percent real cost reduction that Marvin requested. Marvin and Ray agreed to seek the remaining cost reduction from better portfolio management that is already under way (make more money by doing only the right things). Equally important, they have also shortened product launch cycles by 90 days and strengthened the sales team's ability to generate revenue from new products. Let's examine the benefits that Ray was able to harvest:

1. Programs are planned and executed more effectively using the project collaboration environment, reducing cost overruns as

problems are identified and solved early—before they cause substantial rework and incur additional costs.

2. Team members are selected wherever they are available and work effectively with minimal travel. This reduces the expense of hiring contractors when an equally skilled employee is available at another location.

3. Planning, execution and collaboration between departments, even when they are not co-located, is at an all-time peak in effectiveness, resulting in an average 20 percent (90-day) improvement in the product release cycle. This gets products into revenue production sooner and reduces the cost that would have been incurred when the elapsed time for the project went longer.

4. Planning and collaboration with suppliers is equally effective, virtually eliminating rework cost and product design delays due to communication failures with suppliers.

5. Global product launches work better than ever before because international sales and marketing teams can be made part of the core product team and participate fully in international product specifications and international marketing programs. Also, the international teams are fully up to speed on the product by the time it is ready for launch. The result is higher growth in international revenue and cost savings on internationalization of products because it is built in from the first day of program and product design.

6. Employees aren't as likely to leave the company due to lifestyle decisions or a spouse's job change. In the first 18 months, this has allowed Ray to keep four key employees whose departure would have cost almost $400,000 in recruiting and training fees, with substantially greater impact on their projects.
7. The company was able to make four acquisitions and they used their approach to virtual teaming to attract two companies that would have been uninterested had they been forced to move to a corporate campus. They were able to integrate the acquired companies faster and more effectively than before, saving several hundred thousand dollars in integration costs.

So, did everything work like magic? Of course not. What hard lessons did they learn?

1. Not every manager can manage a distributed team. It is a learned and practiced skill, just like any other management and leadership skill.
2. When problems came up on distributed teams, the dispersion was often used as an excuse to cover up basic weaknesses. A strong leadership team can plan, execute, assign and supervise work and resolve problems as effectively as a team under a single roof. When Ray looked carefully at the problems, he found that the most disciplined teams succeeded locally, learned and succeeded in the distributed environment.

3. Not every remote employee has the discipline or motivation to achieve the level of productivity that they achieved in a traditional workplace. Some employees need the structure of the workday to stay focused on the task at hand. By measuring results rather than attendance, Ray learned to focus on what made employees successful. Those that produced poor results ultimately left, whether they were remote or local.

4. Remote locations need a strong leader. A weak leader, or one who has not bought into the corporate culture can actually cause harm. By being remote, acquired teams can often fall into the feeling that they operate just the same as they always did and never become part of the company. Success is completely about leadership. Some acquired leaders blended nicely into the corporate culture. Others needed to be replaced for the integration to be successful.

The problems that Ray and Sandra found and solved during the project were there all along. The distance brought them quickly to the surface and forced the company to deal with them. In the end, they not only benefited from the economics of running a virtual team, they also became more disciplined overall, which set them on a path to continuous improvement.

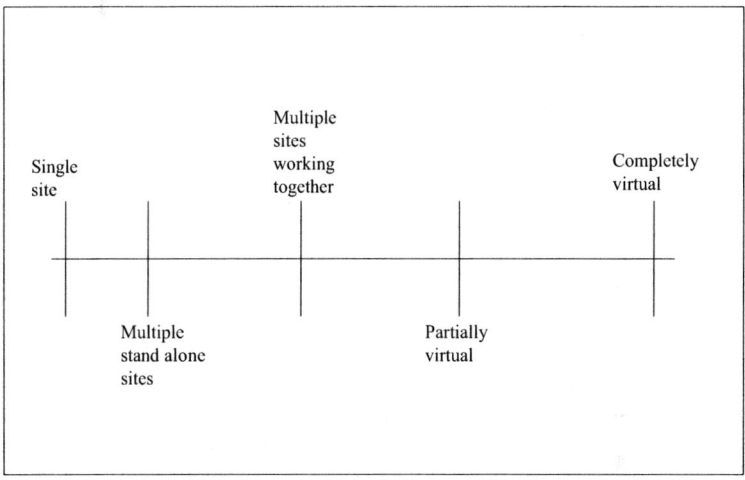

Every organization has a choice about where to live on the virtual continuum. To attempt to live completely to the left at a single site is to choose denial. It simply ignores the existence of customers and suppliers, the economics of a global labor force and the fact that most companies have a field sales and service organization that must be a part of projects, whether they are the launch of a new product or the creation of a new information technology solution.

By contrast, Li's fictitious company, Indonesian Medical Technologies, is probably further to the right on the virtual spectrum than most product companies can move at this time. It is a good place for consulting companies, auditors and other service companies because they spend most of their time at the customer site and go to the office infrequently. It is also a good place for companies like the business analyst community because it allows them to leverage "world class experts" wherever they find them in roles where they create independent research.

The technology for running virtual companies has matured to the point where it is no longer the barrier to becoming a completely virtual company. High-speed communications, project collaboration databases, electronic meeting centers, PC-based video, electronic whiteboards and instant messengers are the complete set of technologies necessary to operate in a virtual world. Other technologies will be added that make things better, but the base technology set exists today. Virtual private networks are effective enough that security is not a major issue for most remote workers, or even between suppliers and customers.

The remaining changes to make this work are business practices and social norms. People love progress, but they hate change. It will take a conscious effort to change the business practices and make them stick. It is only worth the effort if it is done for the purpose of achieving measurable economic returns. But the necessary changes for business practices will happen over time. Every organization has some level of remote operations and they will need to adopt technologies and business practices similar to those outlined in this book to address those remote operations.

How Virtual Should You Be?

The final frontier is social norms. In the 1970s and early 1980s we established the number of hours that a person worked in the office, or the number of miles that a person flew for business as measures of success.

- Can you be power player if you get up at six in the morning, work at your desk, have a leisurely breakfast with your family and get to the office at 9:30? How will you ever convince people that you're still putting in 12-hour days?
- It seems less impressive to find a customer problem, assemble a virtual team and solve the problem in a few hours or days while continuing with your personal life as normal, even though you can be in touch with your team and your customer, plan and execute work and even assign and personally supervise the work, all without getting on a plane.
- And besides, if we learn to be there without going there, how will we ever live on fewer airline miles?

Perhaps we need to make **results** the *new definition of success for the 21st century*. No matter how much we give a person to do, it always gets done and it always gets done well and on time. And amazingly, they are only in the office seven or eight hours a day or four days a week. Perhaps they are peddling furiously from home the other five hours a day, but only the people who look at the results and the timesheets will ever know.

The best companies are learning to run their businesses by being there without going there. They are using their travel time and budget to brainstorm, build relationships and spend time talking about those things that are really better said in person. They are recruiting the best and the brightest wherever they find them and they are genuinely taking advantage of the 24-hour-a-day business clock and the economics of a global labor force. They are finding that it can be hard, but that the rewards are measurable and go straight to the bottom line.

See you in a virtual workplace soon—perhaps sooner than you think.

About the Authors

George Van Ness is the CEO of Business Engine, a software company that builds technology to enhance the productivity and financial control of project-based organizations such as Information Technology, Engineering and R&D. The company's flagship product, the Business Engine Network (The BEN), gives teams the visibility and control they need to manage across time zones, geography and corporate boundaries.

George began his career in the Big 5 consulting firms doing large systems integration. As a partner at both KPMG and as the U.S. leader of the information technology practice at Coopers & Lybrand, he was a thought leader in the creation of the large-scale Systems Integration practices and sponsor for product development and project management methods and quality programs.

In 1993, George moved to the software industry as a Group Vice President for the Central U.S. Services practice at Oracle Corporation where he was a member of the leadership team that moved Oracle from after product support services to systems integration. He then moved to product development to run industry development teams in Oil & Gas and Consumer Packaged Goods teams where he began to focus on running large distributed product development teams in San Francisco, London, Paris, Houston, Denver and India, while integrating software from 5 international software firms. The unique challenges of that environment, plus his subsequent experience as the leader at Business Engine have led to the principles advanced in *Being There Without Going There*.

Keith Van Ness is an MBA candidate at the Southern Methodist University Cox School of Business. He has an undergraduate degree in mechanical engineering from the University of Missouri. He also has experience in marketing, finance, engineering, product development, and distributed and virtual business practices.

Keith began his product development career with EDS in a unique program on cross-functional processes and organizations. He worked for a major auto manufacturer developing embedded controls software. In this role, he led teams in the United States, India and Japan responsible for testing the software for the project.

Keith and George bring a unique multi-generational combination to the distributed virtual business model. Keith's currency as an operating line manager and George's 25 years of experience as a consultant and software executive bring a broad perspective and create a unique writing team.

ASPATORE
C-Level Business Intelligence™

Publisher of Books, Business Intelligence
Publications & Services
www.Aspatore.com

Aspatore is the world's largest and most exclusive publisher of C-Level executives (CEO, CFO, CTO, CMO, Partner) from the world's most respected companies. Aspatore annually publishes C-Level executives from over half the Global 500, top 250 professional services firms, law firms (MPs/Chairs), and other leading companies of all sizes in books, briefs, reports, articles and other publications. By focusing on publishing only C-Level executives, Aspatore provides professionals of all levels with proven business intelligence from industry insiders, rather than relying on the knowledge of unknown authors and analysts. Aspatore publishes an innovative line of business intelligence resources including Inside the Minds, Bigwig Briefs, ExecRecs, Business Travel Bible, Brainstormers, The C-Level Test, and C-Level Business Review (Magazine), in addition to other best selling business books, briefs and essays. Aspatore also provides an array of business services including The C-Level Library, PIA Reports, SmartPacks, and The C-Level Review, as well as outsourced business library and researching capabilities. Aspatore focuses on traditional print publishing and providing business intelligence services, while our portfolio companies, Corporate Publishing Group (B2B writing & editing), Aspatore Speaker's Network, and Aspatore Stores focus on developing areas within the business and publishing worlds.